God
Said It...
and Bang!
It Happened

D1050851

Bruce & Stan's

God Said It... and Bang! It Happened

The UnBelievable Explanation of Creation

Tommy nelson™
Thomas Nelson, Inc. • Nashville

You may contact the authors via e-mail at
guide@bruceandstan.com or send letters to:

Bruce & Stan
P.O. Box 25565
Fresno CA 93729-5565

Text copyright © 2001 by Bruce Bickel and Stan Jantz
Illustrations copyright © 2001 by Bill Ross

All rights reserved. No portion of this book may be reproduced in any form without
written permission from the publisher, with the exception of brief excerpts in reviews.

Published in Nashville, Tennessee, by Tommy Nelson®, a division of Thomas Nelson, Inc.

Scripture quotations are from the *Holy Bible,* New Living Translation,
copyright © 1996. Used by permission of Tyndale House Publishers, Inc.,
Wheaton, Illinois 60189. All rights reserved.

Library of Congress Cataloging-in-Publication Data
Bickel, Bruce 1952–
    God said it and—bang! it happened / Bruce and Stan.
      p. cm.
  ISBN 0-8499-7613-8
    1. Creation—Juvenile literature. 2. Theology, Doctrinal—Juvenile literature.
  [1. Creation.] I. Jantz, Stan, 1952- II. Title.
  BT695 .B45 2000
  231.7'65—dc21   00-048947

Printed in the United States of America
01 02 03 04 05 PHX 9 8 7 6 5 4 3 2 1

Contents

Introduction

Questions. Life is full of them, and you've probably got a lot of your own.

* Some are *frivolous:* If you stick a bean up your nose,
  will it grow roots into your brain?
* Some are *practical:* Should you keep buying VHS tapes,
  or will DVD soon make them all obsolete?
* And, some are a bit *fanciful:* How do you decide between
  your competing career ambitions of professional soccer player,
  Internet business tycoon, and pop music star?

For most of the questions that you have, the answers turn out to be pretty insignificant (except bean roots in your brain could be somewhat painful). Your worries about VHS will be forgotten when your new

DVD collection becomes outdated. And you'll have a little different perspective on career goals when you discover that your parents—when they were your age—hoped to be astronauts or professional disco dancers (and you probably want to avoid that last mental picture).

We'll admit that we don't know you very well (after all, we've only been acquainted with you for about 179 words or so), but we suspect that you have a few other questions—questions that are much more than just frivolous, practical, or fanciful.

If you're intelligent (and we suspect that you are because, hey, you're reading this book), you probably have a few philosophical questions. Like questions about whether the Bible makes sense. Oh sure, you've heard the Sunday school lessons about God creating the world in six days, but you're probably curious about a lot of stuff that isn't mentioned in the creation story. You're probably wondering:

* **Why aren't dinosaurs mentioned in the Bible?** (After all, they're the stars in a few blockbuster movies, so why isn't there a single verse about them in the Bible?)

* **What about the cavemen?** Is that what Adam really looked like, all hairy and slouched over? (And does that mean Eve was really hairy, too?) If the cavemen were some form of sub-humans, why doesn't the Bible talk about them?

* **And, is there life on other planets?** Did God only create us humans, or is there intelligent life somewhere else in outer space? Does the Bible give any clues about space aliens?

See, we told you there are lots of questions. But there's more. What about:

* **Does Science agree or disagree with the Bible?** Why do some Bible teachers say the world is 10,000 years old but most scientists say the earth is about 10 billion years old? Who is right? Who is wrong?
* **What should you do in science class if the teacher starts talking about how the world began?** Do you start reciting Genesis 1:1 ("In the beginning God created the heavens and the earth"), or do you just keep your mouth shut? What if someone says that humans "evolved" from the monkeys?

Doesn't it boil down to this one simple question:

Is the Bible's explanation of creation believable?

Now, you might not want to ask that question in church (because you're afraid the pastor would hit you on the head with a hymnal), but it is an honest question. God won't get mad if you ask it. In fact, we think He wants you to ask questions like that.

We're writing this book to help you go "behind the scenes" of the creation story. Sort of, "Creation: Up Close and Personal." We'll be covering some awesome stuff:

* **Outer space!** (planets and solar systems and asteroids and meteors)
* **The earth!** (volcanoes and earthquakes and floods)
* **Where humans came from!** (Don't confuse this with the "Where do babies come from?" question. We won't be talking about the mechanics of human reproduction.

In this book, we're looking at how humans got on the earth. If you have questions about human sexuality, you'll have to look in another book. Or, you can ask your parents about it—but be prepared for them to act kind of nervous and weird.)

We're going to be talking about some serious stuff, but we promise you that it won't get boring. (We hate to write dull stuff as much as you hate to read it.) So, nothing boring; just the really cool facts. They might seem unbelievable at first, but when you put them all together, it's totally believable!

Oh, by the way, we are biased. (Most authors won't admit that. They all want to seem objective, but all writers work from their own viewpoints, and their opinions influence them. But we've had this growing friendship with you—up to about 771 words now—so we want to be completely honest with you.) Here is our bias:

We believe the Bible is absolutely and entirely true.

That means we'll be going to the Bible as our #1 source of information about the creation of the world and the human race.

Now, we aren't two brain-dead, nonthinking Christian morons who believe the Bible just because some screaming preacher in a white polyester suit on cable TV told us to. We believe the Bible because we put it to the test and found it to be true. We'll take the same approach with you. We'll tell

you what the Bible says, we'll compare it to history and to modern science, and we'll let you decide for yourself. (You won't hear any screaming preaching from us. And the only white polyester suit you'll find is in your dad's closet with his old disco clothes.)

We've got one final confession to make: We are going to be telling you a lot about the Bible and a lot about science. But we didn't get all of this information from our own minds. We aren't that smart because our brain capacity is rather limited. (Hey, we had to learn the answer to the "bean in the nostril" question the hard way.) But we have done a lot of research to learn what other people—with larger brains—have discovered. We have talked to a lot of scientists and religious folks, and we have read the books by the ones we didn't get a chance to talk to. (We're sure they *wanted* to talk to us, but they must have been too busy in their laboratories and their pulpits.) We digested a lot of information, and we have regurgitated it in this book. We won't be asking you to believe what *we* say; we're just giving you the information so you can decide for yourself.

Now, before you begin reading Chapter 1, we just want to make this one last point:

Your Life is going to be a lot better when you realize that the Bible's explanation of creation is totally believable.

Don't misunderstand us. Your school locker will still get stuck, the gym teacher will still yell at you for running too slow, and you'll still give a dumb answer in math class every once in a while that everyone will laugh at. But you won't have to hide your head in your lunch bag when your teacher or the other students start talking about how the world began. You'll be an expert, and you might even know more about this subject than the teacher does. (You can thank us later.)

Stan

Bruce

Chapter 1

How Why Begin at the Beginning

Help us out here. We're going to make a pretty bold statement, and we need your help to decide if it's true. Here goes:

Everything has a beginning.

Is this true? Seems like it would be, but let's put it to the test in three different categories. Decide if everything in each category has a beginning.

* **Stories** — Does every story have a beginning? Let's say someone began a story by saying, "Once upon a time." Does that mean once upon a time *in the beginning?* Not necessarily. Let's say you once had a neighbor named Britney, and you wanted to tell a story about her. You would begin your story with,

6

"Once upon a time, Britney lived next door to me, but then she moved away to become a teen idol." Your story wouldn't be the beginning of Britney's life. It would be just one part of it. It would only be the beginning of your *story* of Britney. In this sense, all stories have a real beginning—whether you're reading a book, seeing a movie, or watching a play.

✹ **People**—Does every person have a beginning? Let's go back to Britney. Even though your *story* about Britney didn't start at the beginning of her life, Britney's life definitely had a beginning. She was born somewhere, she grew up in a family, she moved next door to you for a while, and then she moved away. Although you don't know how Britney's story is going to end, you know that her life had a beginning.

The same goes for all people, including you. If you're living, you definitely had a beginning. (Hey, even if you're dead, you once had a beginning. For anything to exist, it must first begin.) You were born somewhere, and before that (say, about nine months before), your parents conceived you. Before that moment of conception, you didn't exist. Your life began because someone took some action. In fact, every living thing on this earth got here because someone or something did something to bring that life about. Life doesn't pop up by itself. All life has a beginning.

✹ **Stuff**—What about inanimate objects, like the book you're reading? How did this book get here in your hands? More important, how did this book come to exist in the first place? Did it suddenly appear as if by magic, or was there a process involved? Of course, there was a process. We came up with the idea, Tommy Nelson decided to publish the book (suckers), and then someone arranged for a whole bunch of trees to be chopped down so the book could be printed. Just like your story about Britney had a beginning, and your life had a beginning, this book and all the stuff in the world had a beginning. Stuff doesn't just happen (not even the stuff that gets you into trouble).

What about the Universe?

So far we've been talking about everyday things—Britney, you, this book. It doesn't take a genius to conclude that all people and things have beginnings. But what about something much bigger, like the universe (which includes everything we've been talking about and a whole lot more)? Did the universe have a beginning, or has it always been this way?

What IS the Universe?

The universe basically includes everything that exists—and we mean *everything*—the earth, space, pimples—you name it, it's part of the universe.

The universe includes the mountains, the oceans, and the deserts. Have they always been here, or did they have a beginning? The universe includes things you can only see with a telescope, like planets and stars and galaxies. Did they have a beginning? The universe also includes things you can only see with a microscope, like molecules and atoms and cells. Did they have a beginning?

It's Easy to Say Yes . . . but Wait a Minute

It would be easy to say yes, the universe and everything—big and small, far and near—had a beginning. It would be easy, and it would be correct (we'll find out why a little later). However, just because it's easy and correct doesn't mean you shouldn't know *why*. Knowing *why* the universe and everything in it had a beginning is critical, because it takes you to the question of *where*, as in—

Where Did the Universe Come From?

As well as the question of *how,* as in—

How Did It Happen?

These are critical questions to answer! And now is a great time to learn the correct answers (before someone gives you the wrong answers). Knowing where the universe came from will help you answer those other perplexing questions about life, such as "What happens to those socks that get lost in the dryer?"[1]

Have You Ever Thought about Being a Cosmologist?

The study of the universe is called *cosmology,* not to be confused with *cosmetology,* which is the study of hair. You could be a *cosmologist* who practices *cosmetology* on the side, but we wouldn't recommend it.

Why, Where, and How?

Let's first figure out *why* the universe had a beginning, because that will lead us to *where* it came from and *how* it happened. It's going to take the rest of this chapter and the rest of this book to answer the *why, where,* and *how.* Can you hang with us? If you can, then we guarantee that you will not only know where the universe came from, but you will know where you came from as well (and we're not talking about Springfield or Cleveland).

---

1. No one really knows what happens to those lost socks, but we have a theory. We believe there is a parallel Sock Universe inside your dryer where single socks wander around looking for their mates. It's rather sad.

In the Beginning

A little earlier in this chapter, we said that for anything to exist, it must first have a beginning. Why is that such an important question, especially where the universe is concerned? Well, if the universe had a beginning, guess what? There had to be something or someone to begin it!

This is called *the principle of cause and effect*, which goes like this:

Every effect has a cause.

You are an effect, Britney is an effect, this book is an effect, and the universe is an effect. All of these effects must first have a cause.

The Case of the Throbbing Thumb

Here's a simple science experiment to show you how the principle of cause and effect works in real life.[2] You will need three things in order to conduct your experiment: a hammer, your thumb, and earplugs. Once you have collected these items, carefully follow this procedure:

1. Insert the earplugs.
2. Pick up the hammer.
3. Strike your thumb.

You will quickly discover that the hammer is the *cause* of your now-throbbing thumb, which is the *effect* (your pain and your screaming will also be effects).

---

2. We interrupt this test to bring you a very important message: This is a joke. It is only a joke. Do not actually try this at home, silly person.

If effects don't have causes, then you are left with some pretty ridiculous options. Let's use you as an example (we'll give your poor thumb a rest). If you didn't have a cause, there are only three other possibilities:

1. You don't exist. This is easy to deny. If you are here, then you exist. You could be a rock or a rock star. It doesn't matter. Your being here means you exist. And if you exist, you are an effect, and if you are an effect, you have a cause.

2. You have always existed. If you think you have always existed, then you are either delusional or you are God. Since there's only one God, nobody else can be God, not even you on a really good day.

3. You created yourself. Okay, now we're getting into a weird area. You could claim to be self-created, but there are at least two people (your mother and the person who delivered you) who would contradict you, because they witnessed your birth. Even they wouldn't claim to have created you. As Bruce's mother once told him, "I brought you into this world, and I can take you out." Your mother carried you, but she didn't create you, and neither did you create yourself.

Now let's use the same reasoning with the universe. If the universe didn't have a beginning, then there are only three other possibilities:

1. The universe doesn't exist. This is a "well, duh" kind of argument, but we'll say it anyway. It's impossible for the universe not to exist, because by its very definition, the universe includes everything that exists. Since it contains everything that exists, the universe has to exist. Another way to look at it is like this: If the universe didn't exist, then nothing else would exist either, and the whole issue wouldn't matter.

2. The universe has always existed. Now, this is an interesting idea. A lot of very smart people used to believe that the universe has always existed in a "steady state." This idea was also known as the "continuous creation theory."

The Steady State Universe

The universe had no beginning but rather existed in a steady state condition with new matter being formed from that which was already there. According to the theory, the universe has existed in this way throughout all time.

The problem with this theory is that during the last century, scientists have made discoveries in astronomy, physics, and chemistry that proved the steady state theory to be completely wrong. An astronomer by the name of Edwin Hubble (you've heard of the Hubble telescope) found dramatic proof that the universe definitely had a beginning, and he proved it with an older theory by another pretty smart guy, Albert Einstein, whose research backed up Hubble's finding with the theory of relativity (more about that in Chapter 3).

3. The universe created itself. You can't create yourself, and neither can the universe, because if you have nothing to begin with, you can't make something. There's a little Latin phrase that goes:

Ex Nihil, Nihil fit.

That means, "From nothing, nothing comes." Think about that for a minute. Besides impressing your friends with a foreign language phrase (especially a *dead* foreign language), you can impress them with your logic. You can't get something from nothing. End of story.

The Fourth Possibility

But the universe had to come from somewhere. If it exists now, and it hasn't always existed, and it didn't create itself, then where did it come from? Ah, now you're getting the picture. Now you know why it's so important for the universe to have a beginning. Because if the universe had a beginning, then something or someone had to begin it. This is what we call:

The First Cause

There had to be a beginner, or a First Cause. Without a First Cause, you have nothing, and you can't get something from nothing. But because we have something (that would be the universe and every-thing in it), there must have been something there before the universe that caused the universe. More important, that something had to be *self-existent*. In other words, it had to always exist. And if something had to be self-existent, then What or Who is it? To put it another way, What or Who is the First Cause?

Are you with us here? This is really, really important. Now you're thinking at a pretty deep level (sorry to get so deep this early in the book, but it's important to think this through before we go on to the other stuff). If you can grasp this, then you are ready to think through just about anything (which can come in very handy in all sorts of situations).

Why Does There Have to Be a First Cause?

Everything in the universe has a cause. As you go back further and further in the "chain of causes," you must come to a First Cause that got the whole thing going. Without the First Cause, nothing else (including you) would exist.

So What or Who Is the First Cause?

When it comes to the First Cause, there are only two choices:

Choice #1 — The universe is the First Cause, which means the uni-verse caused itself.

Choice #2—God is the First Cause, which means God caused the universe.

Let's look at each of these choices. The first choice is dumb, but the second choice makes sense.

The Reason Choice #1 Is Dumb

We have already said that the universe can't create itself, and it can't cause itself either. Let's go back to your throbbing thumb. The effect of your throbbing thumb could cause a chain reaction, resulting in other effects (in response to your throbbing thumb, you could fall, knock over a lamp, causing an electrical short that eventually burns your house down, all because you were silly enough to participate in our science experiment).

Your thumb, like the universe, can cause effects, but it can't be the First Cause. Your thumb, like the universe, can't just swell up and throb all by itself without some First Cause (which in this case happens to be the hammer). Without the hammer, your thumb and your house would be perfectly safe.

The Reason Choice #2 Makes Sense

Since the universe (or your thumb, or any other effect) can't be the First Cause, we have no choice but to accept God as the First Cause. There are no other choices. Why is that? Because God is the only being who ever lived who is *self-existent*.

What It Means for God to Be Self-Existent

God has no beginning and therefore no cause. By definition, every *effect* must have a *cause*, but God is not an effect. He has always been, and He will always be. God does not need outside support to exist. This is what is meant by *self-existent*. King David understood this when he wrote:

Before the mountains were created, before you made the earth and the world, you are God, without beginning or end. (Psalm 90:2)

As we're going to find out in Chapter 3, most scientists now agree that the universe had a beginning, and they even believe that something began it. Where they disagree is *what* that beginning (or First Cause) was. Many scientists and science teachers who believe in the beginning of the universe refuse to refer to the First Cause as God. "Why does it have to be God?" they ask. "Why can't the First Cause be an impersonal force?"

While this thinking pattern is certainly the right of every person on this earth, the evidence in our universe (as you're going to see throughout the rest of the book) points to a God who is not only self-existent, but also—

Eternal
Higher and Greater than us
Personal
Loving

In the next chapter, we're going to take a closer look at this God who created the universe. Can we know Him, and if so, what is He like? What kind of personality does He have?

So WHat?

It would be easy to say, "So what's the big deal? Why is it so important for the universe to have a beginning, and why is it so important for God to be the First Cause? What difference does that make in my life now?" It makes a huge difference. Here are a few reasons:

You can know where the universe came from and how it happened (stay tuned). You don't have to believe that the universe came here by accident or by chance. You can put your faith in a personal God rather than some kind of "impersonal force" or "cosmic energy."

You can trust the Bible, because the Bible is the only "holy book" that correctly describes how the universe began (again, stay tuned).

You can believe that God the First Cause has unlimited capabilities, and that He chooses to use His power for your benefit and your future.

Chapter 2

What's the Big Deal about God?

You've got to admit it: God is pretty popular.

* He has a huge fan club—with millions of members—
  that has existed for thousands of years (that would be the
  people who have believed in Him).
* He has His own book (the Bible), not to mention
  all the thousands of books that other people
  have written about Him.
* He has people recording songs about Him on CDs
  and talking about Him on cable television
  (although He doesn't get mentioned too often on MTV).

And perhaps most amazing of all, even the people who don't
believe in Him (that would be the *atheists*) spend a lot of time talking

about how He doesn't exist. In fact, sometimes the people who *don't* believe in Him want to talk about God more than the people who *do* believe in Him.

Let's face it. God is controversial because so many people have different opinions about Him. These different beliefs can easily turn into arguments:

* The atheist says: "God doesn't exist, and I dare you to prove that He does."
* The person who believes in God replies: "Well, He does exist, and you can't prove that He doesn't."

Those kind of arguments aren't going to do anything for anybody (except maybe get you red in the face).

You've Got Nothing to Be Afraid Of

Many Christians back away from discussions with people who are skeptical about the existence of God. These Christians don't want to find themselves in an argument about whether God exists because they're sure they will lose. Oh, they believe in God and know that He exists because they feel Him at work in their lives. But they are afraid that they won't be able to prove God *to someone else* who can't see Him, feel Him, or hear Him. But you can be a hero and come to their rescue because you know what to say when talking with someone who is skeptical about God (or if you don't know already, then you will after you've finished reading the next few pages).

Don't Get Stuck Carrying the Burden of Proof

Actually, there is evidence that God exists, but before we go there, let's talk for a moment about who carries the *burden of proof* in any argument about God. You know about the concept of "burden of proof" from watching lawyer shows on TV. (We're assuming you don't yet have *personal* experience with criminal proceedings.) When you watch criminal court-room dramas, notice that the prosecution (the government) has the burden of proof:

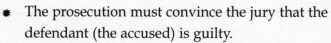

* The prosecution must convince the jury that the defendant (the accused) is guilty.
* If the prosecution doesn't present enough convincing evidence to "prove" that the defendant committed the crime, then the defendant is declared "not guilty" and walks away (usually to commit another crime shortly after the next commercial).

In our criminal justice system, the prosecution has the *burden of proof* because the defendant is presumed innocent until proven guilty.

When it comes to discussions (or arguments) about the existence of God, most everyone (including Christians) assumes that the Christian has the burden of proof. They start with the presumption of atheism: that God does not exist. In other words, they assume that a belief in God is irrational until enough evidence is presented to persuade a skeptic. But that is the wrong presumption.

Instead, begin with this presumption: God exists, and a belief in Him is rational until enough evidence is presented to the contrary. That shifts the burden of proof to the skeptic (or atheist) to prove that God doesn't exist. Now who is on the hot seat?

We know what you are thinking:

Shifting the "burden of proof" is easy to say but difficult to do.

You're also thinking:

Of course Christians want to start with the presumption that God exists, but why should an atheist or a skeptic start with that presumption?

Oh, we are so glad that you asked that question (and you should be glad, too, when an atheist or skeptic asks it of you). Don't worry about the fact that God can't be seen or heard. Evidence of His existence can be observed, and based on that evidence, reason and logic suggest that a belief in God is very rational.

Shifting the Burden of Proof

If you want to know how this burden of proof and presumption thing works, try this test on one of your friends. (It's perfectly safe—no hammers or fires.) When you are eating lunch at school, ask your friend if his mother exists. After your friend makes an expression like he just swallowed a moth, he'll say, "Sure!" This is your cue to say: "Well, prove it."

Because his mother will be nowhere in sight (assuming she's not a teacher at the school), your friend will be stuck because there is nothing he can do to make you see her or hear her. And it doesn't prove his mother exists if he shows you his peanut butter and jelly sandwich with the bread crusts cut off—that just means he has a wimpy sandwich. (Even though we know bread-crust-chopping is only a mom thing, it doesn't prove she exists. Although it does suggest your friend is kind of a mama's boy. Tell him to be a man and eat the crusts.) But you see what we mean. He knows she exists; you know she exists; but proving the obvious may be difficult if you start with the wrong presumption.

Believing in God Is Very Logical, and You've Got the Arguments to Prove It

Don't be afraid to start any discussion about God with the presumption that He exists. It is totally logical. And just in case you need them, here are four famous arguments for God's existence. (We didn't make them up. They were already famous before we came along. And we even have a tough time pronouncing them, so we have given them nicknames.)

1. The Cosmological Argument (the "Cosmic Dominoes" argument).

The fact that the world exists requires some explanation. Yes, our world and the greater cosmos seem to be humming along by themselves, but something had to get them started. We like the dominoes illustration used by philosophy professor Ronald H. Nash to explain this concept. You've probably seen one of those "World's Most Worthless Wonders" television shows with an elaborate arrangement of dominoes sitting on edge across a gymnasium floor. When a single domino is pushed, it starts a chain reaction of falling dominoes, each tipping over the other, until the whole thing displays a mosaic of Abraham Lincoln's face (or something equally spectacular but perhaps more attractive). Now, the dominoes didn't start falling by themselves. The first one was pushed. And the finger of the person that pushed that first domino was "the first cause."

As we will explain in greater detail in Chapter 3 (where we give you some scientific statistics), our cosmos is so complicated that it had to have a first cause. It had to have something to get it started. (And any argument that all of the cosmos just fell into place by itself is as illogical as saying that all of those dominoes arranged themselves on the gymnasium floor.)

2. The Teleological Argument (the "Designer Label" argument).

The cosmological argument deals with the *existence* of the world, and the teleological argument deals with the *design* of the things in the world. The obvious orderly design in the universe (from the solar system to your digestive track) implies that there was a Supreme Designer involved in the process.

Professor Nash has another great illustration for this argument. Imagine that astronauts exploring the moon discover a working camera. Further imagine that this isn't some piece of space junk that fell off the deteriorating Mir space station, and it isn't some piece of tourist litter from a previous astronaut. Nope, this is a highly sophisticated piece of photographic equipment that wasn't made by human hands. The newspaper headlines would be declaring intelligent life in outer space, the world's armies would start taking defensive measures, and Jerry Springer would be interviewing someone who claimed to have dated the alien Giant Brain.

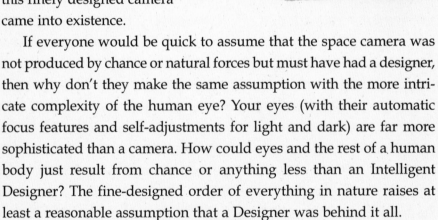

It is obvious that complex, complicated mechanisms don't happen by themselves, so there has to be some explanation. An Intelligent Designer is the best possible explanation for how this finely designed camera came into existence.

If everyone would be quick to assume that the space camera was not produced by chance or natural forces but must have had a designer, then why don't they make the same assumption with the more intricate complexity of the human eye? Your eyes (with their automatic focus features and self-adjustments for light and dark) are far more sophisticated than a camera. How could eyes and the rest of a human body just result from chance or anything less than an Intelligent Designer? The fine-designed order of everything in nature raises at least a reasonable assumption that a Designer was behind it all.

3. THE ONTOLOGICAL ARGUMENT (the "Up Close and Personal" argument).

If God doesn't exist, then how did we ever get an idea about Him? The ontological argument supports the existence of God because there has been a notion of God ever since the beginning of the human race. (Even if a person rejects the notion of Adam and Eve in the Garden of Eden, archaeologists have found evidence of worship dating as far back as 8,000 to 24,000 years ago.) The constant belief in God through the ages gives some proof to His existence.

THe SuRVey SayS . . .

Surveys consistently show that the majority of Americans believe that God exists and that He was involved in the creation of the world.

Here's an analogy. We know that there is a gravitational pull from the moon that causes the earth's ocean tides to rise and fall. We can't see the tug of gravity, but we can see its effects. So, too, we can't see God, but in every generation of humanity some people have felt a tug to move toward Him.

A related argument focuses on the actual experiences that people have had with God. We aren't talking about wackos who claim to be God — we are talking about normal, clear-thinking people who claim to have a personal experience with the Almighty God. Over the centuries, there have probably been millions and millions (maybe billions) of such people — including us and probably you. A few of these people might have been mistaken (and misinterpreted God for what was really just a bad case of indigestion). But have *all* of them been wrong? If billions of people have had a notion of God, the presumption that God exists isn't a far-fetched, freaky idea.

4. THe MoRaL ARGuMeNt (the "Did I Do That?" argument).

Have you ever felt guilty for doing something that you knew was wrong — even though no one told you not to do it? Have you ever been angry because you thought someone else's conduct was wrong? In every human society, there has been a "moral code" that sets the standard for acceptable (and unacceptable) behavior.

Animals don't have a moral code. Your dog may *look* like he feels guilty when makes a puddle on the carpet. He may hang his head and hide from you, but that isn't from guilt. He's just afraid of being swatted on the nose with a newspaper. He may not "puddle-ize" your carpet again, but that is not his way of saying, "I'm sorry." It is just his 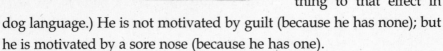 way of saying, "My nose gets swatted every time I do that, and I don't like getting my nose swatted, so I won't do that again." (Or something to that effect in dog language.) He is not motivated by guilt (because he has none); but he is motivated by a sore nose (because he has one).

Guilt is a human emotion that comes from a built-in moral compass. Where did that come from? The fact that we acknowledge a set of standards for right and wrong suggests that we are accountable to a higher power. We know that there are consequences to our acts.

A few people may argue that there is no real code of morality. They say that cheating and lying are wrong only if you impose that arbitrary standard on yourself. They say that people should decide for themselves what they want to do. If they think there is no God, they often believe there is no universal moral code that applies to everyone. You can shut these people up pretty quickly if you steal something that belongs to them. (Money always works well.) All of a sudden they'll have a moral code that they feel should apply to you.

The existence of God's influence appears to be present when we acknowledge a moral code that we can't live up to. We all have faults and failures, yet we aspire to a moral code that sets a higher standard. If there were no God, and if we were left to design a moral code just for ourselves, don't you think we'd set a lower standard that we could easily satisfy?

Belief in God Is Reasonable

These arguments don't provide conclusive proof of God's existence. There can be objections to any one of them. But whether you take them individually or as a group, you've got a very logical basis for believing that God exists. Don't be intimidated in any discussion with a skeptic about God. With these four arguments, your belief in God is totally reasonable. Make the skeptics carry the burden of proof. After all, when these arguments are considered, the one who denies the existence of God seems illogical. (Of course, this means you'll probably have to read the last few pages again to make sure you understand the arguments. You can't just say, "God exists because of Cosmic Dominoes." And you can't say "ontological" to most people because they'll think you're referring to that stomach gas that makes you burp.)

What Kind of God Is He?

The arguments we just reviewed show that it is reasonable to believe in God. But those arguments don't really tell much about the nature of God—just that He exists. And the scientific facts that we will review in the next few chapters just show that there was an Intelligent Designer involved in the creation process; those facts don't really reveal much about His nature or personality.

So, even if you believe that God exists, you might not know much about Him. Well, that isn't enough, bucko. If you are serious about answering the "Where did I come from?" question, then you need to know about the character of the God who created you. You have to know about His personality because it reveals His attitude about what

He created (that would be you), and how that creation (that would be you, again) should respond to Him. Here's what we mean:

* What if God is just an impersonal natural force (as in "Mother Nature")? Then your "creation" into this world doesn't have any more significance than when droppings from a flying bird fertilize a seed on the ground that grows into a plant.
* What if God is a master designer who makes stuff and then leaves (like a kid who builds a sandcastle on the beach and then walks away)? Then it looks like He left you to fend for yourself.
* Or, is God like an ancient great-great-grandfather who was really powerful thousands of years ago but who is now just feeble and forgetful? Then He doesn't have much to offer you.
* What if God is like a permissible grandmother — you know, the kind who will give you whatever you want so long as you act sweet and loving? Then you can look forward to living a phony life if you just want to get lots of stuff.
* Have you ever worried that God might be a really mean tyrant who wants to punish you whenever you are having fun? If that is the case, then you better plan on a boring life or else keep an eye out for bolts of lightning.

Do you see what we mean? If you believe that God exists, and that He created you, then you'd better find out about His personality. That's the big deal about God. If you are part of His grand design, you better find out what He thinks about you and what He expects from you.

What's in a Name?

Most names are pretty bland and don't tell you much about the person. (Bruce and Stan are excellent examples of dull names. If the name is going to be descriptive, it usually belongs to a WWF wrestler

like "the Exterminator" or "Gut Monster".) But it wasn't always this way. Years ago, in Bible times, names had great significance. And God had quite a few names because it took a lot of names to describe His many characteristics.

We can Learn about God from His various names:

Father: God assumes the role of a loving father and considers us to be His children. (You can kiss your worries about a tyrant goodbye.)

Jehovah: This Hebrew term literally means, "I Am that I Am." It means that God is everything that we need.

Lord: This is a term of respect (much like we would refer to someone as "sir" today). It emphasizes that God has authority over all of us and deserves our worship.

Elohim: This is another Hebrew term that describes God as being strong and powerful.

God: We hear you saying, "Duh!" But don't overlook the obvious. In the Greek language of the New Testament, this word (*theos*) means "the one true God." It implies that God is unique, that He is the Creator, and that He is the Savior.

If You Want to Know More . . . You Can Read His Biography

Finding out more about God's personality isn't difficult. In fact, it's easy. Don't forget that the Bible contains sixty-six separate books, written over a period of about 1,500 years . . . and it's all about God.

You can trust what the Bible says about God because He inspired the authors to write what He was saying about Himself.

Here are just a few of the insights that you can learn about God's nature, character, and personality by reading the Bible (and we're giving you some verse references that you can look up for yourself):

* **GOD IS Omniscient:** He knows everything (Psalm 139:1–4). He knows what happened in the past (because He was there), He knows what is happening now, and He knows all about the future. If you need an answer, you can go to God.

* **GOD IS Omnipotent:** He is all-powerful (Revelation 19:6). There is no force on earth, or in heaven, that is mightier than God. In any celestial battle with the forces of evil, He will prevail. If you are in trouble, you need God.

* **GOD IS Omnipresent:** He is everywhere at once (Psalm 139:7–12). Maybe that's why nothing happens that He doesn't know about. This means that you can never run away from God. But it also means that wherever you go, He will be with you.

* **GOD IS Immutable:** He never changes (Malachi 3:6). Aren't you glad that the One who designed the program for the universe isn't going to change the rules on you? He isn't grouchy on "bad days" and doesn't get stressed out. You can depend on God.

* **GOD IS Love:** This is the one that everyone is counting on (1 John 4:7–9). We *expect* that a God of love will be totally forgiving and let us get away with anything so long as we say "I'm sorry" before it's too late. Well, God *is* love. God wants to keep you as a friend even when you're a real jerk. (But don't think that God's loving character outweighs the other features of His personality. Keep reading.)

* **GOD IS HOLY AND JUST:** He is perfect and demands that sin be punished (1 Peter 1:15–16; Deuteronomy 32:4; Romans 6:23). This is bad news for the people who think God is going to be lenient. God enforces the rules even if punishment is involved. (But His loving character has provided a way for your sins to be forgiven because the penalty—which He still requires—was paid by Jesus.)

Perception Is Reality: Seeing Where You Came from Depends upon How You See the World

Now that we have briefly examined the character traits of God, we have a better understanding of who He is. So when we talk about whether God exists, we know that we are **NOT** talking about:

* A little potbellied, cupid look-a with wings and a silly grin who flits around from person to person spreading good luck. (Don't laugh. Some people really believe that.)
* A distant, impersonal space alien is too busy with intergalactic wa asteroids to remember us measly on this tiny planet.
* A cranky, old grump who wants to stomp on you whenever you're having a little fun (kind of like the cafeteria lady).

Nope. He is an all-powerful yet loving God who wants to be our heavenly Father. You can't get much more personal than that.

Knowing that God exists and knowing about His personality is REALLY BIG STUFF. Whether you realize it or not, these thoughts affect how you live, and the decisions you make, and how you feel about what happens to you. In other words, how you view the world is determined by what you believe about God. (Not surprisingly, this is called your "world-view.")

So What?

Basically, there are just two world-views: one with God and one without Him. Let's think about these two opposing world-views for a moment. Look at where each belief will take you.

In a World-view without God:

* The universe in which you live came from nothing; it just happened.
* No one is in charge.
* Your life has no significance; it just happened.
* There is no master plan.
* Your life has no meaning.
* You can live how you want because it really doesn't matter.
* When you die, that's it. Game over.

On the other hand, look at the completely different results when you believe in God (the One with the personality traits as described in the Bible).

In a World-view that includes God:

* He created the universe in which you live.
* As the Creator, He is in charge.
* As one of His creations, your life is important and significant to Him; in fact, He loves you.
* The whole world (that includes you) is part of His master plan.

* You better find out about His plan for the world (that includes you).
* Nothing happens that He didn't already know about.
* Your actions have spiritual significance because they either go along with His plan or they go against it.
* There is an eternal, spiritual aspect to life; your physical death isn't the end of you.

You see, God's incredible process of creating the world (and you) is a big deal. It is not just a simple question of how the world began; it is also a question of the value and significance of your life. And it makes a big difference in what you do with your life. Knowing how you got here may help you decide where you are going to end up in the future.

But let's not get sidetracked with looking to the future right now. Let's look at how things got started. To do that, we have to go back to the beginning. In fact, in Chapter 3 we will go back to *before* the beginning.

Long, Long Ago in a Galaxy Far Away

It's one thing to have a world-view, and another thing entirely to *believe* it. Your world-view can include God (and we hope it does), but unless you really believe it's true, the way you live probably won't be all that different from the person whose world-view doesn't include God.

Very few people would say they don't believe in God, but a lot of people who claim to believe in God act as if He doesn't matter. They tell you, "Yeah, I believe in God and that He created the world and all that stuff." But they don't believe God has a plan for the world and a plan for them. So they live every day from their own viewpoint rather than from the viewpoint of God, the Creator of the universe.

You Better Believe It

* Do you believe in God?
* Do you believe that what God says in the Bible is true?

Those are two different beliefs, you know. It's easy to believe in God (hey, even the demons believe in God—see James 2:19). What's not so easy is to believe that what God says in His Word is true. This is where some people have problems because God says a lot of stuff that makes them uncomfortable. Or the Bible explains things in a way they just can't accept.

Take the beginning of the universe, for example. The Bible is really simple when it talks about how the world began. So simple that some people believe it's all a fairy tale. "You tell me the universe was created in six days?" they ask. "Ridiculous! Don't you know that the universe is billions of years old? How can I believe the Bible if the first chapter is all wrong?"

And so you sit there with your arms folded and your lower lip stuck out, and you say, "I don't care what the scientists say. They're wrong! I'm going to believe the Bible when it says, 'In the beginning God created the heavens and the earth,' and that's all there is to it."

Truth is, you don't have to be defensive about how the world began. You can believe what God says in His Word—because it's true. And you can believe what science says—as long as it's true (sometimes scientific theories turn out to be false). If the science is true, you don't have to be afraid that it's going to contradict God. God is the source of truth, so nothing that is true is going to go against Him.

So What Does This Mean for You?

* You aren't using some "crutch" to get through life.
* You don't have to put your brains in a drawer and shrug your shoulders when someone asks you about your faith.
* You don't have to walk into science class and cower in the corner because your teacher has

the truth and you've got some kind of mythical, mickey mouse belief.

Science: Good or Good for Nothing?

Science is neither good nor bad. It simply observes what God made. Scientists look at stuff to see if there is a way to measure it—the temperature, the time, the speed, the weight, the frequency. Then they try to find out if the measurements are consistent or repeatable. They do this by conducting experiments (kind of like you did for your school's science fair). Scientists come to conclusions based on the evidence.

The Universe Points to God

Besides believing in God and believing what He wrote in His Word, you've got something else to go on. You've got the stuff God made—His creation. As you're going to see, the whole universe points to God. Here's what the Bible says:

> *The heavens tell of the glory of God. The skies display his marvelous craftsmanship. Day after day they continue to speak; night after night they make him known.* (Psalm 19:1–2)

King David wrote those words 3,000 years ago—before they had telescopes or microscopes or any scopes scientists today use to observe and measure stuff. Back then you had to take God's Word for it. Today, we still take God's Word for it, but we have a big advantage. Because we have telescopes and microscopes and all kinds of scopes and sophisticated instruments designed to measure the universe and everything in it, we can see the actual evidence that God made the world. And the more science learns, the stronger the evidence becomes. You can take this to the bank:

The more we learn about how the universe began and how it works, the more the universe points to God.

If God is in your life, then you have truth on your side. Believe it! God is the First Cause, not some made-up spirit. God is the Creator, not something people created. He was there in the beginning because He *is* the beginning. In fact, God was there *before* the beginning.

God and Science

What we're going to do now is look at how God brought this universe into existence. And to do it, we're going to briefly study some amazing discoveries scientists have made in the last few years that confirm what the Bible says about the world and how it got here.

Please understand: science currently cannot prove God exists because science can't put God in a laboratory and dissect Him. What science can do is give you the confidence that what the Bible says about the world is reliable. It's called evidence. So, don't dismiss science in your journey to get to know God better! And don't think for a moment that science is your enemy or the enemy of God. That's ridiculous. God created science when He created the world. He loves science—even if some scientists don't believe God exists.

And Now a Word from God

Let's review what Chapter 1 said about the beginning of the universe:

* The universe exists but has not always existed.
* The universe had a beginning, and therefore a First Cause.
* The universe can't create itself.
* The Creator (or First Cause) of the universe is God.

Now we're going to find out how God did it. How did He create the universe? The Bible offers a big clue when it says:

> By faith we understand that the entire universe was formed at God's command, that what we now see did not come from anything that can be seen. (Hebrews 11:3)

This is really significant. The Bible says that God made the universe from nothing, and He did it by commanding it. God literally spoke the universe into existence. "Wait a minute," you might be saying. "Now you're going back to fairy-tale stuff. What do you mean, 'God spoke the universe into existence'?"

Hey, God didn't need some gigantic cosmic oven where He made the universe like a chef bakes a cake. He's God. He's all-powerful, all-knowing, completely beyond us and what we can see. All He had to do was say it . . . and BANG it happened!

A Single Point in Time

Edwin Hubble conducted a series of experiments during the mid- to late 1920s. He pointed his telescope at distant stars both within the Milky Way (our galaxy) and beyond, discovering other galaxies. He then measured the speeds and distances of different galaxies. He found that other galaxies are moving away from our galaxy at increasingly rapid rates. He correctly concluded that since all galaxies are moving away from each other, they used to be closer together.

To get a clearer picture of what Hubble meant, think of yourself as the universe for a minute (this time it's all of you and not just your thumb). Since the day you were born, you have been expanding physically in all directions. Even though this doesn't sound very complimentary, you have gotten more *vast* (just like the universe).

Now, your expansion means that at one time you were smaller, even smaller than the cute little baby you once were. In fact, you were once so small that it would have taken a microscope to see you (no doubt you were a very cute microscopic being). That was your beginning (just like the universe).

Einstein Gets into the Act

When Hubble began his work at Mt. Wilson Observatory, Albert Einstein was refining his general theory of relativity, which also had to do with the beginning of the world. Hubble's later discovery strongly confirmed Einstein's theory that there had to be a beginning, and Einstein himself became very interested in how God created the world.

God and the Big Bang

Now we're getting to the core of this book (that's why we put it in the title). Maybe this is why you decided to read this book. You've heard about this thing called the "big bang," and you wonder if there's anything to it. Is the big bang simply a way to take God out of the picture and process of creation, or does it describe something that happened "long, long ago in a galaxy far away"? If it happened the way scientists say it did, was God involved in it? More important, did God cause the big bang?

The short answer is *yes*. Here's how it happened.

What Is the Big Bang?

Basically, the big bang is a way for science to explain how the universe began. Dr. Hugh Ross, an astrophysicist, explains that all the matter and energy in the universe exploded from a point much smaller than the period at the end of this sentence (about the same size you were when you began). Of course, this is where any similarities between your beginning and the beginning of the universe end. Your little beginning was pretty quiet. On the other hand, the universe literally began with a BANG! That little point smaller than a period contained a near infinite amount of density, temperature, and pressure.

Since Hubble and Einstein, most scientists have believed that the universe began in an instant of time with a fierce explosion of pure energy. This pure energy altered itself into forms of matter. John Wiester, a physical scientist, explains that the big bang instantly produced subatomic particles called neutrinos and particles of light called photons. These were followed in the blinking of an eye by electrons, positrons, and neutrons. The initial temperatures of the universe were beyond comprehension.

Did God Use the Big Bang?

Actually, God didn't use the big bang at all. He *created* the big bang. The big bang is the best description we mere mortals can give to the beginning of the universe. The Bible's description is much simpler and more elegant. Here's how the Bible describes the big bang, the point of creation, the First Cause:

> Then God said, "Let there be light," and there was light.
> (Genesis 1:3)

Oh man, was there ever light! This wasn't like flicking on the light switch in your room. It wasn't like turning on the floodlights at a stadium. This was the greatest explosion of light and energy the universe has ever known. The big bang was so powerful that scientists are able to measure its heat . . . *right now!*

We're going to say that again because it's the most awesome evidence ever for the beginning of the universe and the way it happened. Scientists are still able to measure the heat of the big bang. The effect of God's words, "Let there be light," can be observed today!

The Discovery of the Century

On April 24, 1992, an American research team led by George Smoot, an astrophysicist from the University of California at Berkeley, announced that it had used the Cosmic Background Explorer (COBE) satellite to measure the "ripples" of heat from the beginning of the universe. Scientists from around the world were impressed. In fact, they were stunned. Why? Because the COBE measurements literally confirmed the big-bang creation event. George Smoot said: "If you're religious, it's like looking at God."

The Effects of the Light

"The universe was created at the sharply defined beginning of time in a fiery explosion of dazzling brilliance," Wiester wrote. When God said, "Let there be light," He created all the energy, forces, and particles needed to fill "the immensities of space with gases, elements, stars, and planets."

You'll find this explanation in your science books at school, but you won't find any mention of God. Instead, you'll hear that all this happened by "chance," or that an "impersonal force" caused the big bang.

Well, chance never created anything. All chance can do is tell you how likely it is that something will or won't happen (such as you getting an A on your biology final if you don't study). As for the "impersonal force," that just doesn't cut it either. Dr. Ross points out that most astronomers now attribute the beginning of the universe to a supernatural deity. Dr. Smoot wrote: "The big bang, the most cataclysmic event we can imagine, on closer inspection appears finely orchestrated."

An impersonal force doesn't orchestrate anything. Throw a bunch of impersonal metal, rubber, plastic, and glass on the ground, and you will never see the day (no matter how long you wait) when the raw material assembles itself into a Ferrari. If you want a car, you have to design and build a car. If you want a universe, someone really powerful and way beyond us has to design and build it. The only "someone" capable of doing that is God. And only God is purposeful enough and loving enough to intentionally design it for our benefit—right here on earth.

In order to make a universe as big and wonderful as it is, lasting as long as it is — we're talking fifteen billion years and we're talking huge distances here — in order for it to be that big, you have to make it very perfectly.

—George Smoot

WHeN WaS tHe BeGiNNiNG?

One of the biggest differences between people who believe God created the universe and those who don't has to do with *when*. In other words, *when* did it begin? That's a tricky question, because none of us were around back then—whether it was 10,000 or 10 billion years ago.

The scientific evidence seems to point to an old universe—say 10 to 15 billion years old. On the other hand, the Bible doesn't say when the universe was created. It just says, "In the beginning God created the heavens and the earth."

Is the Universe Young?

Many people who believe God created the universe are absolutely sure that the "beginning" was about 6,000 years ago. People who hold to this view are called "young earth creationists."

Where Did the Young Earth Idea Come From?

The young earth idea came from a guy who lived in the seventeenth century. His name was Bishop James Ussher. To come up with the "beginning" he counted the generations (also known as "genealogies") listed in the Bible. He started with Jesus, who was born around 3 B.C. (B.C. means "Before Christ," and A.D. means "Anno Domini," which is Latin for "the year of our Lord," which is kind of like saying, "the year the Lord was born"), and then counted the generations back until he got to Adam. Bishop Ussher figured that the world began around 4000 B.C.

The problem is that since Bishop Ussher made his calculations, Bible scholars have concluded that the Bible doesn't include *every* generation. Setting dates based on the number of generations listed in the Bible isn't totally reliable.

Not only do young earth creationists believe in a young universe, they also believe the universe was created in six literal twenty-four-hour days. As you can imagine, most scientists (including your biology teacher) don't believe in a young universe or in six literal twenty-four-hour days. If you were to walk into your biology class and say, "You guys are wrong—the universe is only 6,000 years old, not 10 billion, and it took God only six days to do it," you would make a lot of people laugh. They would be convinced that you believe in creation rather than evolution.

Is the Universe Old?

On the other hand, if you were to walk into most churches and say, "You guys are wrong—the universe is 10 billion years old, not 10,000, and God took a long time to create everything"—you would probably get a lot of people upset. They would think you believe in evolution rather than creation.

So you've got this dilemma:

* If you believe the universe is young, you're branded a "creationist" by science.

* If you believe the universe is old, you're branded an "evolutionist" by the church.

A Practical Approach

Do you see what's happened here? "Creation" has come to mean "young earth," and "evolution" has come to come to mean "old earth." That just isn't so.

* "Creation" simply means "God was the First Cause, the Intelligent Designer, the loving Creator." It doesn't mean "God created the earth 6,000 years ago."

* "Evolution" simply means "change." It doesn't mean "The universe came from nothing and all things evolved from a bunch of goop."

God *could* have created the universe in six literal days, and it *could* have happened 6,000 years ago. (He also could have created the world in six minutes and done it 60,000 years ago.) But God also *could* have created the universe 10 billion years ago and taken several billion years to do it. He's God, and He can do *anything* He wants!

God and Days

The Old Testament (that's where you find the book of Genesis) was originally written in the Hebrew language. One of the characteristics of Hebrew is that the same word can mean different things depending on the context. The word *day* has at least three different meanings:

Sunrise to sunset (twelve hours)
Sunrise to sunrise (twenty-four hours)
A *longer period of time*, sometimes called an *age* or *epoch*

When the Bible says "day" when it talks about creation, it's not clear which definition is the correct one. Maybe that's why Moses, who wrote the book of Genesis, also wrote this directly to God:

For you, a thousand years are as yesterday! They are like a few hours! (Psalm 90:4)

Besides the issue of *when*, there's the issue of *why*. Why would God allow His created beings (that's us) to discover more and more about His created universe, only to be wrong about the whole thing? Why would science, which God created when He created the world, point people away from God? Psalm 19 says, "The heavens *tell of* the glory of God," not "The heavens *contradict* the glory of God."

So What?

We don't think you have to choose between alienating your teacher and upsetting your pastor. You don't have to compromise your beliefs in God and your study of science. Don't get hung up on the *when*. Instead, concentrate on the *Who* (as in God) and the *how* (as in how did it happen). That's what we're going to do throughout the rest of this book.

We're also going to write from the viewpoint that God created the universe several billion years ago, because we believe science points to an old universe, and it doesn't contradict the Bible. You can call us "old earth theists" (we'll call you that, too, if you want).

We're not scientists, and we're not theologians. We're just two ordinary, practical guys trying to make sense out of all this. We want to present the facts of the Bible and the facts of science as best we can. We hope it helps you as you continue reading.

God's Next Big Step

According to Genesis, God made the universe on the first day of creation, but He wasn't finished. Far from it! The next thing God did was to turn His attention to earth, that big blue marble we call home. In the next chapter you're going to see that God made the earth "just right" for His created beings.

Chapter 4

Getting Down to Earth

(And We're Not Just Talking about UFOs)

In Chapter 3, we got you a universe to live in. (Okay, *we*—Bruce and Stan—didn't. God did. But at least we told you about it in Chapter 3.) That was a pretty good start, considering that there was nothing before that. But not just "any old place" in the universe is good enough for you. Oh, no! You need something much more specifically designed for your special, even fragile needs. After all, you are a human (despite occasional references to the contrary made by your parents when describing your table manners or the mess that is your bedroom). And as a human, you must have certain conditions, or you can't exist.

In this chapter, we're going to look at Days 2, 3, and 4 of creation. Those are the days when God got the earth ready for occupancy by you and all the other living things.

Planet Earth: A Goldilocks Place for Life

When we left off at the end of Day 1 of creation, God had big-banged the earth into existence. But don't think that God arranged the billions and billions of stars and planets in an "eenie, meenie, minee, moe" fashion. Each was put in a specifically designed place and position. That is particularly true of the earth's place in our solar system.

You see, you couldn't live on the earth unless it was "just right." Pardon our choice of fairy-tale character, but you are a lot like Goldilocks in this regard. Life wouldn't be possible if the earth were too hot, or too cold, or too little, or too big. Nope. It has to be "just right." If planet Earth had been placed in a different galaxy, or in a different place in our solar system within our galaxy, then life could not survive on it.

If Earth were a bit closer to the sun, we would all burn up. If Earth were a bit farther away from the sun, then we would all freeze to death. (Or if the earth were a bit larger—with more mass—then we would be crushed to death by its gravity.) Let's face it, whether you are charred, freeze-dried, or flattened, it's not a great way to live. God knew that, so Earth was positioned perfectly by God for you (and your Goldilocks-like requirements).

Why the Earth Is "Just Right" for You

God's intentional design of Earth as *your* planet is pretty obvious. It didn't happen by accident that you are here instead of anywhere else. And while there are times when you might wish you were living on another planet (because you want to be as far away as possible from your annoying younger siblings), there isn't any other place that you could go. Look at how the earth is perfectly fitted as a place for you to live:

* The earth is almost 93 million miles (149,573,000 km) from the sun. At that distance, it is "just right" for life. In fact, Earth is the only planet in our solar system just the right distance from the sun to provide enough oxygen so you can do that little thing you always like to do—called *breathing*. If the distance of the earth from the sun were just 1 percent farther away, then glaciers would have covered the earth about 2 billion years ago. The oceans would have frozen, and the temperature of the earth would be less than 50 degrees *below* zero Fahrenheit (–46 Celsius). Does the phrase "chilled to the bone" come to mind?

* And it wouldn't get any better if Earth were closer to the sun. Venus is closer (about 67 million miles or 107,500,000 km from the sun), but it has an atmosphere that you might consider too hot. A miserably hot day here on Earth might be about 115 degrees Fahrenheit (46 Celsius), but on Venus, the temperature gets to be about 860 degrees Fahrenheit (460 Celsius). If that isn't enough to discourage you from moving closer to the sun, then maybe we also ought to mention that it rains sulfuric acid on Venus.

* If the orbit of the earth around the sun were only 5 percent smaller, then we would have a huge "greenhouse effect" in our atmosphere, and the oceans would boil. (It takes all the fun out of surfing when the water melts the skin off your bones.)

* If the size of the earth were smaller, it wouldn't have enough gravitational pull to hold water vapor in its atmosphere. If you wonder what life without water would be like, think about a planet that has the consistency of the ashes in your fireplace. And a smaller mass wouldn't have enough gravity to hold on to its present atmosphere, especially the oxygen. (How long can you hold your breath?)

* You can't have the earth too much larger either. An increased

mass would have a greater gravitational attraction that would hold a heavy, smog-like cover in our atmosphere (containing harmful gases, like hydrogen, methane, and ammonia), and we would be stuck with an environment similar to Jupiter's (and that is why Jupiter is not a popular tourist attraction).

* There would be other more serious problems if the earth were larger. For example, if the earth were twice its current size, then the gravity would be stronger and everything would weigh eight times as much. (Picture yourself at 720–960 pounds or so. Pretty hard to climb stairs when you are packing that kind of weight around.)

* If the earth were much smaller or much larger, the temperature variations would make the earth uninhabitable. Let's face it. You probably complain when your house thermostat is off by two degrees. Imagine how miserable you would be if the temperature were about 100 degrees too cold or too hot for you. Playing soccer on Saturday morning would turn you into a petrified ice sculpture or a puddle of melted flesh. Either way, it's hard to kick a soccer ball.

* The earth's atmosphere and magnetic field act as a type of shield that protects you from damaging radiation and meteors. (If you wonder if that protection is important, take a look at the moon. Those craters are the result of meteors that hit the moon because it doesn't have a protective blanket like Earth's. Aren't you glad you don't have to worry about having one of those craters on your head?)

* The crust of the earth is just the right thickness. Think of it like a pizza. If a pizza crust is too thin, then you can't hold it up and the toppings keep falling off (usually onto your lap). If the crust of the earth were thinner, there would be many more earthquakes, and volcanic activity would be erupting around the world, maybe in your backyard. (Molten lava flowing

through your bedroom is a much bigger problem than grease stains on your lap.)

* If the earth didn't spin as it orbited the sun, we couldn't live. Half the earth would have too much sun, and the other half would be in darkness (so half the world's population would be fried to a crisp and half would be frozen to death). The result would be similar if the earth rotated, but at a slower rate than once every 24 hours. Venus rotates at the rate of once every 243 days. (Now that is *sloooow*. Imagine a "night-time" being about twelve weeks long. You'd get a good sleep, but you'd need it because a "school day" would be about 1,800 hours long.)

* The earth is tilted about 23 degrees on its axis. We need both the *spin* and the *tilt* to give us our four seasons (and don't forget that the spinning gives us *day* and *night*). If the earth weren't tilted and spinning, then many places on Earth would be uninhabitable because the temperatures would be extreme (very hot or very cold) all year long. Many types of plant and animal life couldn't survive because they need the change of temperatures that comes with the changing seasons. (Oh, we know what you are thinking. An endless summer would be great. But maybe you would get stuck with a perpetual winter. Snow is fun, but not if you have to shovel it every day for the rest of your life, and you know that is exactly the household chore that would get dumped on *you*.)

You might think that there have to be a lot of other planets in the universe where atmospheric conditions are suitable for life. We can understand why you might think this. The universe has about a billion galaxies, and each galaxy has countless stars—hundreds of millions to even more than a trillion. That means that the number of solar systems for you to choose from is huge (like 10, followed by 20 more zeros). But most of these other solar systems have to be ruled out:

* You can't live in any solar system that has more than one star. (These are called "binary" or "multiple star" systems.) You need to live on a planet that has a circular orbit, and planets in binary or multiple-star systems orbit in an ellipse instead of a circle. (Earth's only star is the sun. Because the earth orbits in a circle, it is always the same distance from the sun. This avoids drastic weather patterns that would occur in an elliptical orbit that is sometimes much closer to, and sometimes much farther away from, the center star.) This fact alone rules out about two-thirds of all other solar systems.

* You can't live in a solar system that has a star smaller than our sun. The planet would have to orbit closer in order to be livable (where water could exist as a liquid), but then the tidal forces would slow the rotation and the planet would cook. (And you'd be stuck living on a planet like Mercury—where the midday temperature is hot enough to melt lead.)

* And you must rule out every solar system that doesn't have larger planets than the one you would be living on. We've got several larger planets in our solar system. Earth's diameter is about 7,926 miles (12,755 km). That's huge if you're planning a hike around the Equator, but it is rather puny compared to Neptune (about 30,760 miles/49,503 km), Uranus (about 32,000 miles/51,499 km), Saturn (about 74,500 miles/119,896 km) and Jupiter (about 88,736 miles/142,806 km). These larger planets are necessary to knock most of the asteroids and comets out of the way that would otherwise smash into Earth. Think of these larger planets like the windshield on your car. If the bugs didn't splat on the windshield, they would be splatting on your face. It would hurt a lot worse if an asteroid

bashed you on the head. So if you are going to move to a different solar system, you have to find a livable planet that has a few other bigger planets around it to block out the falling space debris.

When they consider the atmospheric conditions that must be "just right" to sustain life, some scientists calculate that only a trillionth of a trillionth of a percent of all stars would have a planet in their solar system that you could live on. That is 0.0000000000000000000001 percent. Basically, that means you couldn't expect that even one planet, by natural processes, would be suitable for you, personally, as a carbon-based life form. So, what do you think about all of this? Did you just luck out, or did God do you a huge favor by specifically designing the earth to meet your needs?

What about extraterrestrials and UFOs?

At times, God may wonder if there is intelligent life on *this* planet. But we know that you are probably wondering about whether life exists on other planets. Maybe you've been wondering about this question for a long time. Well, wait no longer. Here is the answer:

NOBODY KNOWS FOR SURE.

Okay, we know that wasn't the answer you were hoping for. You probably wanted something a little less wishy-washy. Sorry. Nobody can tell you for sure. But we don't want you to be so frustrated that you try to shred this book in your mother's food processor (because there are some good chapters left that you haven't read yet). So, we aren't going to leave this "life in outer space" question so quickly. Let's think it through together by asking (and answering) a few basic questions:

1. Is it possible that God created life on other planets? Sure. He is God. Anything (and everything) is possible with God.

2. Is there any evidence that God created life on other planets? None yet. Bible scholars don't find any mention of extraterrestrial life forms on other planets mentioned in the Bible. And scientists have been trying to make contact with intelligence in outer space (such as the SETI [Search for Extraterrestrial Intelligence] Institute projects), but so far nobody (or no thing) has responded.

3. If there is life in outer space, where could it exist? Think back about the factors we have reviewed for human life to exist on planet Earth. (It was only a few pages ago.) Those factors and conditions are also applicable when we consider the possibility of extraterrestrial life forms. If you define *life* in terms of what we know it to be (for humans, animals, and plants), then many scientists believe that life on other planets is improbable because similar atmospheric conditions don't exist elsewhere.

4. But what about all of those UFO sightings? People see lots of weird things in the sky. Most of the time, there is some logical, rational explanation for what was seen. (That "giant head of a space alien" turns out to have been a hot air balloon.) Often, when there isn't an explanation, it turns out that the "sighting" was nothing more than an intentional hoax, an attempt to get attention, or just a very vivid imagination. These "sightings" never involve physical evidence left behind that can be examined.

5. Is every single UFO incident a fake? Maybe not. But flying saucers might not be the explanation. Let's remember that our world is filled with spiritual forces. God's angels and Satan's demons are at work on our planet.

If the subject of space aliens fascinates you and your friends, here is something amazing to think about (and it will give you a chance to talk to your friends about God): The Bible actually tells the story of how an alien invaded the world. It wasn't an alien from another planet, but it was an alien from heaven. Jesus Christ, the ultimate intelligence from outer space, invaded our atmosphere and came to Earth about 2,000 years ago. And He did it to rescue the human race from ultimate destruction. At some time in the future, according to the Bible, there is going to be a gigantic, intergalactic war between the forces of God and the forces of Satan. Planet Earth will be the battleground. God will prevail, and all of those who have transferred their allegiance to Him will be rescued. Pretty amazing, huh! That true-life story is better than the plot of any science fiction movie.

How God Made Earth "Just Right" for Life

Scientists have been able to determine that the earth was not always suitable for life. It became livable only after a progressive process that spanned billions of years. This process matches perfectly with the sequence of Days 2, 3, and 4 of God's creation in chapter 1 of Genesis. Here is the sequence according to both science and the Bible (and we have thrown in some approximate time frames to help you keep your chronological bearing):

Day 2: Light Breaks Through (beginning about 5 billion years ago)

Let's go back and pick up from where we left off as Day 1 of creation moves into the second day. The big bang got it all started during the Day 1 period about 15 billion years ago. Then it took about 13 billion years for the universe to form with quasars, galaxies, and stars. When the earth was formed, its atmosphere was as dark as ink. There was so much space debris and gases in the atmosphere that the light couldn't penetrate it. But in the Day 2 period, light began to shine through. Not directly, but indirectly. Scientists say that the atmosphere moved from being opaque (light can't pass through) to translucent (diffused light comes through). Scientific theory places the time frame of this Day 2 process in the range of about 3.75 billion years ago to about 7.75 billion years ago.

Here is how the Bible describes it:

> *And God said, "Let there be space between the waters, to separate water from water." And so it was. God made this space to separate the waters above from the waters below. And God called the space "sky." This happened on the second day. (Genesis 1:6-8)*

These verses and science agree. The first significant event to take place in the early history of the earth was the formation of water into the seas and the atmosphere of the sky.

Once the earth's atmosphere became translucent, the process of evaporation started cranking up (you know, that cycle where the waters below—the oceans—evaporate a bit into the water above—the clouds). This evaporation process changed the atmosphere from opaque to translucent. In other words, all of the debris in the air started to clear up, and the light started to come through. But it still

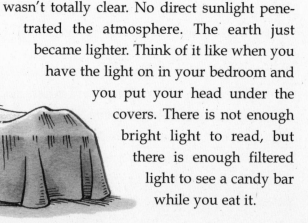

wasn't totally clear. No direct sunlight penetrated the atmosphere. The earth just became lighter. Think of it like when you have the light on in your bedroom and you put your head under the covers. There is not enough bright light to read, but there is enough filtered light to see a candy bar while you eat it.

DAY 3: Land Suddenly Shows, and Plant Life Grows (beginning about 4 billion years ago)

From the very beginning through Day 2, the entire surface of the earth was under water. But there weren't a lot of mountains and valleys back then. The surface (crust) of the earth was pretty much flat, covered by a shallow sea (with the water about 1 mile deep). Then about 3 billion or so years ago, the earth's surface started shifting.

During this Day 3 period, the earth had lots of volcanic activity and earthquakes. These eruptions and quakes caused the surface of the earth to wrinkle (much like your face might wrinkle up at the sight of seeing your dad in a Speedo). When this happened, the land shifted and large masses of land broke through the sea. We guess you could call this a real *breakthrough* event.

This wasn't an event that was out of control. Just the right amount of land was formed. Scientists say that the current ratio of 29 percent land surface to 71 percent water surface is the optimum ratio for life.

This is how the Bible described it:

> And God said, "Let the waters beneath the sky be gathered into one place so dry ground may appear." And so it was. God named the dry ground "land" and the water "seas." And God saw that it was good. (Genesis 1:9)

Geologists have figured out how the land popped up ("appeared") through the seas:

* The center of the earth (its core) is about 2,900 miles (4,630 km) in diameter. There is a solid inner core and a liquid outer core of molten iron and nickel.
* Around the core is a mantle about 1,800 miles (2,896 km) thick, consisting of slightly cooler rock.
* Over the mantle is the earth's crust. Under the ocean, the

crust may be as thin as 6–8 miles (9.6–12.8 km) thick. (While that sounds thick, in proportion it is like the thickness of a coat of paint on a house.) But under our continents, the crust is about 20–25 miles (32–40 km) thick.

* The crust of the earth (under the continents and the seafloor) contains huge solid-rock islands that are called "tectonic plates." These plates are like gigantic rafts (some of them are thousands of miles wide) that "float" on the earth's mantle. These plates move, and when they shift, the surface of the earth moves. The movement of the plates cause all sorts of geologic results, ranging from the formation of mountains to earthquakes and the eruption of volcanoes. (Think of the tectonic plates like a bunch of crackers on top of a pot of bubbling hot chili beans. The earth's crust is like a thin layer of grated cheddar cheese on the crackers. As the chili beans bubble, the crackers shift, and the cheese gets moved around quite a bit.)

Geologists believe that between 2.5 and 4.2 billion years ago, the significant changes of the earth's surface were caused by the tectonic plates that were crashing head-on and rubbing against each other. (Hey! These things are still moving, but you aren't suffering from motion sickness because they are only moving at the rate of about one inch per year. That is the same speed that your thumbnail grows.)

But the appearance of land wasn't the only thing that happened in Day 3. With the evaporation cycle (can you remember back a few billion years to Day 2?) and the appearance of land, plant growth began. The cloudy atmosphere allowed some filtered light in, and that caused a bit of a hothouse effect. That moist, hot atmosphere, mixed with dirt, was excellent for plant growth (kind of like the inside of your running shoes).

The Bible tells it this way:

Then God said, "Let the land burst forth with every sort of grass and seed-bearing plant. And let there be trees that grow seed-bearing fruit. The seeds will then produce the kinds of plants and trees from which they came." And so it was. The land was filled with seed-bearing plants and trees, and their seeds produced plants and trees of like kind. And God saw that it was good. This all happened on the third day. (Genesis 1:11–13)

Archaeologists have found fossil records of life beginning about 3.5 billion years ago with structural traces of "cyanobacteria" which is a primitive type of bacteria and bacteria-like blue-green algae. (These organisms are still found today. Look in the corner of your shower.) Blue-green algae has the capability of releasing oxygen through photosynthesis. After accumulating for about a billion years, mounds of cyanobacteria (called "stromatolites") were flourishing as they floated on top of the shallow-water seas.

The fossil records show that land-dwelling plants appeared about 438–490 million years ago in the form of ferns. Next came seed-bearing plants. The earth was getting ready for animal and human life, but it was still way too dark. (Remember, it's like you in bed with the blanket over your head blocking out most of the light.)

Day 4: Let the Sunshine In (beginning about 2.5 billion years ago)

Even though the earth had plant life growing, three very important (and connected) changes had to happen before the earth would be ready for animal (and human) life:

1. More sunlight was needed as a source of energy.

2. More oxygen was necessary.

3. The dense clouds of noxious smog-like gases that covered the earth had to be removed to make sunlight more visible and to improve the air quality.

All of this happened on Day 4.
Here's the Bible's report:

> And God said, "Let bright lights appear in the sky to separate the day from the night. They will be signs to mark off the seasons, the days, and the years. Let their light shine down upon the earth." And so it was. For God made two great lights, the sun and the moon, to shine down upon the earth. The greater one, the sun, presides during the day; the lesser one, the moon, presides through the night. He also made the stars. God set these lights in the heavens to light the earth, to govern the day and the night, and to separate the light from the darkness. And God saw that it was good. This all happened on the fourth day. (Genesis 1:14–19)

In Day 4, each of the three changes necessary for animal and human life occurred as light broke through the earth's cloudy atmosphere. Scientists place these events during the period of 750,000 million years ago to 2.5 billion years ago. Here's how it happened:

* The earth's rotation rate began to slow. This meant calmer wind velocities. (Jupiter has a complete rotation every ten hours, a rate that is about 2.5 times faster than Earth's. Jupiter has average wind velocities of more than 1,000 mph [which is 1,609 km per hour for you metric types].) With less wind, there was less seawater sprayed into the air, and the cloud cover was reduced.
* The new growing plant life (that little blue-green algae stuff from Day 3) also helped in clearing up the air. Those plants converted carbon dioxide into oxygen (in the process known

as "photosynthesis"). The poisonous gases were transformed into an oxygen-rich atmosphere.

* The result of all this photosynthesis was an ozone layer in Earth's atmosphere. (Actually, it's part of the stratosphere layer that extends from 7 to 30 miles or about 11 to 48 km above the surface of the earth.) The ozone layer filters out the harmful ultraviolet rays and lets in the beneficial rays.

Don't make the mistake of thinking that God created the sun, moon, and stars during Day 4 (although a quick reading of the Day 4 verses might give you that impression). The sun, moon, and stars were already created during Day 1 (and God doesn't have to take any "do-overs"). It is just that the earth's atmosphere became clear in Day 4, so the light from the sun, moon, and stars could be seen from Earth for the first time.

So What?

So, what do you have by the end of Day 4? You've got sunlight reaching the earth. You've got an atmosphere that is filled with oxygen and free from those pesky poisonous and lethal gases. You've got land above the water, and you've got plant life growing. Hey, you're ready for animal life and human life! The only thing holding us up is the arrival of Day 5.

Chapter 5

The Making of Jurassic Park

This is it! We finally got here. The chapter you have been waiting for: the one about dinosaurs. We're sorry that it took four chapters for us to get to this point, but we don't feel too bad about it. Hey, we know that you don't like walking in at the middle of a movie because you don't want to miss how the story begins. Well, now that you know the beginning of the story of creation (Days 1 through 4), you are ready to move ahead.

In this chapter we'll be describing how Day 5 of creation populated the oceans and the sky with fish and birds (and you already know which went where). We'll also talk about the first part of Day 6 when God created animals on the land. Scientists give the Day 5 events a time frame beginning perhaps as long as 750 million years ago, and they theorize that the presence of land animals began about 360 million years ago (as God's timetable moved from Day 5 to Day 6).

As we have done before, we'll look to see what the Bible has to say about it all. But the Bible isn't the only record book that tells us about these stages of creation:

* We also have fossils that give great clues to what happened. Like footprints in the sand at the beach, the fossils leave a record of who (or what) has been there before.
* In particular, we will be looking at dinosaur fossils. Examining dinosaur fossils is important because they can help us fill in a few gaps that the Bible doesn't talk about specifically. (Actually, you won't be *looking* at these fossils; you'll just be *reading* about them. That might not be as much fun as having the actual dinosaur fossils in front of you, but at least you won't have a parent yelling at you for getting fossil dust on the carpet.)

Swimmers and Fliers

When we left off in Chapter 4, we had a great earth—well, great if you are a vegetarian. There was lots of plant life, but nothing yet swimming in the sea, or flying in the air, or walking on the land. Then, all of a sudden, things changed when God spoke on "Day 5."

> *And God said, "Let the waters swarm with fish and other life. Let the skies be filled with birds of every kind." So God created great sea creatures and every sort of fish and every kind of bird. And God saw that it was good. Then God blessed them, saying, "Let the fish multiply and fill the oceans. Let the birds increase and fill the earth." This all happened on the fifth day. (Genesis 1:20–23)*

Now, don't think that God started making these swimmers and fliers one at a time (like popping them out of one of those Play-Doh Factory machines). If He had spent a few minutes handcrafting each one separately, it would have taken millions of years. Actually, this Day 5 covers millions of years, but not because God was behind schedule in His creation shop. Nope, on this day, God was into mass production. Here's what archaeologists have figured out from the fossil records:

* Up until about 600 million years ago, there was plant life happening on earth, but not much else (except for a few simple multicellular organisms that were hanging around since about 700 million years ago). The fossils from that stage show pretty much nothing but ferns and other plants.

* Then about 600 million years ago or so, all of the major invertebrate groups showed up in the ocean. Invertebrates are those squishy things without skeletal structures like worms, jellyfish, starfish, etc. (You'd be squishy yourself if you didn't have any bones.)

* Then, about 540 million years ago, the ocean dwellers with skeletons (coral and shellfish) appeared on the scene. This group includes the crabs and lobsters.

* Later, about 438-490 million years ago, the first living things

with spinal columns—fish—showed up. By about 360 million years ago, larger fish and sharks were thriving. Again, all of this happened in huge numbers and wide varieties.

Scientists have been so amazed by this appearance of numerous life forms in the oceans (what we are calling "swimmers") that they gave a name to this time period. (Scientists are big on giving names to things. And they usually pick some name that makes them appear to be really smart.) They call the period of time beginning 540 million years ago the "Cambrian Explosion." (See what we mean? They couldn't just call it the "Age of Swimmers." Oh, no. That would be way too simple.)

Actually, the term "explosion" fits well. (If you want to demonstrate the scientific principle of *explosion* for your parents, we suggest you violently shake a bottle of Coke or Pepsi and then twist off the cap while you are pointing the bottle at them. You may want them to be standing in the shower in their swimsuits when you try this little experiment.)

When the scientists refer to an "explosion," they are speaking *figuratively* to emphasize that the creatures appeared seemingly at once and out of nowhere. (They don't mean a literal explosion that gives you the mental picture of jellyfish guts being sprayed around the world.)

The ocean wasn't the only place where creation was happening on Day 5. Go back and read the verse on page 61. While God was stirring things up in the water, He also got busy in the sky. And we've got the fossil evidence to prove it. (Well, we don't actually *have* the fossils in our own possession, but we've *seen* them in the museums. And we could have taken them ourselves when the guard was distracted, but we didn't want to set a bad example for you. And we would have looked pretty weird walking out of the museum with a 37-pound slab of sedimentary fossil rock stuffed in our pants.) Here is what the fossil records show about birds and other flying things:

* Geologists have determined that the earliest flying creatures appeared about 286–360 million years ago. These were insects with wings. Based on their body structures, they could only grow to a certain size, but it was much bigger than the kind of insects you are used to. By about 300 million years ago, the cockroaches were about 12 inches long, and the dragonflies had a wingspan of about 24 inches. (Imagine finding one of those insects in your sleeping bag!)
* About 200 million years ago, the insect population started to be reduced by the appearance of a type of flying reptile. (Some of them weren't really good at taking off, but they could glide downward between the trees.)
* Birds with feathered wings showed up between 144 and 163 million years ago. They have pretty much dominated the skies since that time.

So, the fossil records confirm what the Bible says, and they explain a little bit more of the details:

* Day 5 covered millions of years.
* During that time, God created all types of fish and birds.
* After one species would die out, He'd create another.

Up until a few decades ago, most scientists believed that all these varieties of fish and birds evolved from a single invertebrate, and the wide variety of today's fish and birds is just the result of many generations of evolution. But recent discoveries of fossils point to the fact that there are no intermediate developmental stages. There were just invertebrates; then there were the kinds with outside shells; then there were all types of fish and the birds just showed up, too. That's the whole "explosion" part of the Cambrian explosion. Scientists don't call it the "Cambrian Evolution," or even the "Cambrian Slow Transition." All of these creations "exploded" on the scene because God specifically created each type.

CRawLeRs anD WaLKeRS
(anD thin̮g̮S that SLitHeR oN theiR belLieS)

The explosion of life forms on Earth didn't stop with just swimmers and fliers. It includes the period beginning about 400 million years ago when God created animals to occupy the land. This all happened in the first part of Day 6 of creation. (You might say it happened early in the day.) Here is how the Bible describes it:

> And God said, "Let the earth bring forth every kind of animal — livestock, small animals, and wildlife." And so it was. God made all sorts of wild animals, livestock, and small animals, each able to reproduce more of its own kind. And God saw that it was good. (Genesis 1:24–25)

The forty-eight words in those two verses say a lot, but there is a lot more to the story. (Remember, the Bible wasn't designed to be a science book. Its purpose is to tell us about God.) Those verses tell us that God did the creating, and God left fossils and bones to fill us in on some of the scientific details. Here is what is known about the beginnings of animal life on Earth:

* The first creatures to walk (or crawl, or maybe slither) on land were the amphibians. These were critters that could spend a little bit of time out of water, but had to return to it often. They were the main land occupants about 360 million years ago. Don't think that you were born too late and have missed these "water and land" wonders. Just take a look at salamanders and frogs. (And if you take a good look, you'll see that they look a little prehistoric.)

* The next animals to appear on land were the reptiles. Amphibians require both land and water for living, but reptiles can exist completely on dry land. Since the reptiles didn't need to live near water, they could move inland. The "Age of Reptiles" began about 260 million years ago. You can get a pretty good idea about the appearance of these prehistoric reptiles if you look at a few present-day reptiles. (And because you probably don't notice snakes and turtles in your backyard, just watch a few episodes of the *Crocodile Hunter* on cable.)

As with the swimmers and fliers, the amphibians and reptiles were part of an "explosion" of life forms that popped up in lots of varieties all at once. Also, like the swimmers and fliers, some varieties would die out and new ones would begin. But there are no fossils from that period that indicate a major transition where one type of reptile transformed (or "evolved") into a different type.

A Drum Roll, Please . . . The Age of Dinosaurs

There is no specific mention of the word "dinosaurs" in the creation verses of Genesis 1:24–25. Does this mean that the Bible is unreliable? Or, does this mean that all those museum displays of dinosaur bones are fake because dinosaurs didn't really exist? The answer to both questions is a big "NO!" Just think of it this way:

The Bible is reliable (and it can be completely compatible with science) even though it doesn't specifically mention dinosaurs. Genesis 1:24–25 states that God created the "wildlife" and "all sorts of wild animals." These general references certainly include dinosaurs. The verses don't mention any type of animal specifically. (We can't find any verse in the Bible about those little wiener dogs, but no one doubts that they exist or considers the Bible to be unscientific because it fails to mention them.)

Now that we've got that settled, let's look at some fossil evidence to see what else happened during the first part of Day 6 that the Bible didn't mention.

The fossil records show that dinosaurs showed up on the earth about 200 million years ago, and they stuck around for about 140 million years. During that time, the earth was a literal Jurassic Park. These creatures ruled the sky, sea, and land.

Dinosaur is derived from Greek and means "terrifying lizard," and some of these creatures were exactly that. (Try to imagine a very furious lizard the size of Rhode Island.) But they all weren't the types that would crush jeeps and eat children. There was quite a variety of them:

* Some were meat eaters, but others preferred the salad bar.
* Some were very large. The Apatosaurus — what your parents used to call a Brontosaurus — might have been as heavy as 75,000 pounds or 34,020 kg (depending upon whether you weighed it before or after it ate).
* Some were pretty small. The Compsognathus was only about the size of a large chicken.

* There was a wide variety of body styles. Our personal favorite is the Stegosaurus. This is the one that looks like it has a row of shovels sticking out of its back. Those pointy shovel-like plates were probably some type of temperature-regulating device. (They weren't particularly useful in battle—unless the enemy happened to fall out of the air and land on the points of the Stegosaurus's backbone.) For fighting, the Stegosaurus had spikes on the end of its tail, and it would fling its tail against the head or body of its enemy. This tail was a lethal weapon (but it probably wasn't very handy for swishing flies off the Stegosaurus's rear end).

* Not all of these prehistoric creatures were stuck on the ground. Some relatives of the dinosaurs—Pterosaurs—could fly. Some of them were the size of a sparrow; others were as large as an airplane. Scientists used to think that Pterosaurs couldn't really fly but simply glided on the wind to stay in flight. Now it is believed that most of the Pterosaurs could sustain powered flight on their own. The fossils of the Pteranodon show that it had a wingspan of 21 feet (7 m) from tip to tip. (If you are grossed out by pigeon poop, imagine how terrible it would be if you had to worry about a flock of Pteranodons flying over your head.)

So, Where Did All the Dinosaurs Go?

All during the millions of years during and after the Cambrian Explosion, some types of life forms were dying off. But no extinction was as dramatic as what happened to the dinosaurs about 65 million years ago. There is still a lot of debate among scientists about what caused the extinction of the dinosaurs. Some paleontologists think it had to do with gradual changes within the species; others think that it was due to external catastrophes. (We are simplifying the arguments, but you get the idea.) Here are a few points on which both sides agree:

* There were global climatic changes. The environment shifted from warm and mild to a cooler one. There is disagreement about the cause and speed at which these changes occurred.
* There were some catastrophic events as well. Possibly some sort of volcanic eruptions over millions of years. No, the dinosaurs weren't melted by the hot lava. But the volcanic ash and dust thrown into the air could have caused short-term acid rain and the emission of poisonous gases. (What a way to go.) The soot in the air could have had a cooling effect (similar to a nuclear winter), or the long-term effects could have created a greenhouse effect that filtered out the sunlight, reduced plant life (which was food for many dinosaurs), and made the earth too warm.
* The most popular theory is that a comet impacted the earth in an area that is now off the Yucatan coast. As with massive volcanic eruptions, this type of impact would've sent dust and debris into the atmosphere, causing a global "nuclear winter." Darkness and acid rain would have first killed off the plant life, which would've caused the vegetarian dinosaurs to die. Meanwhile, the meat eaters would've slowly run out of prey, until finally, only really tiny animals that burrowed underground could've survived. In various places around the globe, geologists have discovered a thin layer of clay with an unusually high content of iridium (a rare metal similar to platinum) that supports the theory of such a comet impact.

Let's face it. If you are a 75,000-pound Apatosaurus, there aren't too many places you can hide until the climate gets better. And even though the dinosaur die-off debate continues, one thing is for sure: whatever killed them, it did the job.

But Day 6 was far from over! Creation on that day continued for another 65 million years. This is why Apatosaurs didn't see cows,

sheep, or buffalo grazing in the same fields with them. More mammals were yet to come.

Look at What Came Next

Mammals appeared at the beginning of the Jurassic Period (about 208 million years ago), but they were mostly of the small and nocturnal type. When dinosaurs died out (about 65 million years ago), the mammals were able to flourish. (It's easier to multiply when you don't have a Stegosaurus tail knocking you into oblivion.) The Age of Mammals began about 60 million years ago. Within the next 20 million years, the mammals had covered the globe in all the basic types that exist today.

Perhaps you are wondering why the mammals didn't become extinct with the same conditions that killed off the dinosaurs. That's an excellent question. (Even if you weren't wondering, we'll tell you about it.) Mammals were smaller than most of the dinosaurs. Their small size would have made them better able to find shelter against the effects of a nuclear winter. The same is true of the smaller amphibians and reptiles, such as snakes, frogs, and lizards, many of which survived.

Perhaps as many as three-fourths of all living species were killed off by the events that made the dinosaurs extinct. But it was possible for a portion of the mammal population to survive, and without the carnivorous dinosaurs around, the mammal population increased as time went on.

Did God Run out of Ideas for New Creatures?

Day 5 and Day 6 were filled with all sorts of creativity on God's part. New forms of animal life were appearing all the time. You've got to admit that He had a pretty good imagination. (When you think about the giraffe, the zebra, the octopus, the bald eagle, and a mosquito, you realize He wasn't stuck in a creative rut.) So, what's happened now? Why did He stop? Did He just run out of ideas? (When you understand the answer to this question, you'll realize why you keep seeing the same old animals at the zoo, and why there are never any new verses to the "Old MacDonald Had a Farm" song.)

After Day 6, God stopped creating. In fact, the Bible says:

On the seventh day, having finished his task, God rested from all his work. (Genesis 2:2)

We're all living in the Day 7 stage. God's not out of ideas; He has just stopped creating. Oh sure, there are still some slight changes in certain species of animals. There are even slight changes in the species of *Homo sapiens* (that is you and the rest of humanity). For example, on the average humans are taller now than they were a few thousand years ago. But while there are slight evolutionary changes within a species, there are no new species being created. Some are dying out, but no new ones are showing up. God is done creating. (But don't think that He is just loafing around. He is still busy with a gigantic building project, but it is not down here on Earth or in any part of the universe that can be seen. Check out John 14:1–4.)

God Saved the Best for Last

The Bible says that God created the land animals on Day 6. But that isn't all that He did then. Have you noticed that something very important has been left out of the creation story so far? You! Well, not *you* exactly, but your *ancestors*.

God also created human life on the last part of Day 6. It wasn't taken care of when He created the animals. The Bible says that He did it separately. We'll be talking about that in the next chapter. We'll explain why you can dismiss any claim that you share the same family tree with Curious George. And we'll discuss whether cavemen were animals or just people with lots of hair and poor personal hygiene.

So What?

All this "swimmers, fliers, crawlers, and walkers" stuff has some major significance for you:

1. Don't ever think that the Bible is all about God and has nothing to do with biology. While the Bible isn't a science book (so it doesn't give all the details of the creation of the world), God knows His science. The fossil record is entirely consistent with Day 5 and Day 6 of creation as told in Genesis.

2. The order of creation (with swimmers first, then fliers, and then the land animals) on Day 5 and Day 6 is exactly the order that scientists have put them in. If you believe the Bible, then what you believe is exactly the same as what scientists have discovered.

3. You can have lots of fun learning about the dinosaurs, and you don't have to worry about any inconsistencies with the Bible. The dinosaurs are in there (Day 6), but it's just that the names like *Tyrannosaurus rex* weren't mentioned.

4. All of the "swimmers, fliers, crawlers, and walkers" didn't evolve from one life form. There are no fossils that show transitional life forms between the species. The Cambrian Explosion has too many varieties appearing all at once for there to be a gradual evolutionary process. There are no fossil records that show a life form that gradually changed from a reptile into a mammal. There are no fossils that show that the Stegosaurus slowly evolved into the wiener dog (or vice versa). Don't worry about people who spout off differently. They don't know what they are talking about (or they are relying on outdated or unproven scientific theories).

Chapter 6

Monkeys, Cavemen, and You

When you visit a zoo, something strange usually happens. After seeing the cool animals (lions and tigers and bears), as well as the boring ones (gazelles and tortoises and anteaters), you eventually find yourself standing in front of the Primate Pagoda, and you ask yourself a question: Do I and that cute chimpanzee standing by the fence come from the same gene pool, or is he as different from me as I am from my little brother?

There are some striking similarities, especially when the chimp stands upright on two legs. He could pass for your little brother in a dark room. And there are those eyes. The chimp looks at you, and you look at him, and you wonder: Does he see something familiar in me? Maybe he's trying to communicate. Maybe he is my ancestor after all!

Then the chimp goes nuts because some punk standing next to you starts taunting the little guy by throwing peanuts at him. Suddenly the monkey is jumping, screaming, and spitting. You run for cover while peanut boy yells to his slacker friends, "Hey look, Curious George is going psycho!" You might feel sorry for Curious George, but you are pretty sure the two of you don't share the same bloodline.

IS CuRiouS GeoRGe YouR UNcLe?

Later, in biology class, your teacher gives you this very convincing argument for the theory—no, your teacher calls it a *fact*—of evolution. He explains how humans and monkeys share a common ancestor dating back millions of years. He points to a color poster on the wall that shows an ape-like creature on the very left (who looks like your chimp friend), followed by a series of other, bigger monkeys and apes, each one standing more erect than the other. Toward the end of the primate lineup, you notice a guy that looks like a caveman (and a little like Mr. Winchell, your shop teacher). Finally, on the very right of the poster, the progression of monkeys and cavemen finally leads to a guy in a business suit holding a briefcase (who looks a lot like Bill Gates).

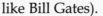

The chart is pretty convincing (although you could do the same thing with the morphing program on your computer), and you begin to wonder about the stuff you were taught at home and at church. Your parents and Sunday school teachers might have had trouble explaining how the dinosaurs and cavemen got here—or if they even existed—and what happened to them. On the other hand, your biology teacher has an explanation, and it sounds pretty good. But you don't want to take God out of the picture, because you believe in Him, so you're kind of stuck. It's like you have to choose between two options, neither of which sounds very good:

Option #1 — Believe what your parents and Sunday school teachers told you (even though they can't explain dinosaurs and cavemen to your satisfaction), because they believe in God and so do you.

Option #2 — Believe your biology teacher (even though he leaves God out of the picture), who says that Curious George is your long-lost uncle.

It's Not a Matter of Either/Or

Hey, we have good news for you. When it comes to monkeys and cavemen and you, it's not a matter of choosing one option or the other, because there is a third way to go. You can believe in God, you can believe in dinosaurs (we already talked about that in Chapter 5), and you can believe in cavemen — because all of that is true. And you don't have to believe that Curious George is your uncle, because that is absolutely false.

As for your biology teacher, we'll deal with him later (check out the "So What?" chapter at the end of the book). The more important thing is to deal with the stuff your biology teacher is teaching (or will be teaching if you haven't had biology yet).

Evolution: Is It Evil or Real?

Evolution isn't something to be afraid of, like some monster under the bed (think back a few years). Evolution happens! (Whoa, before you run out and do something rash like burn this book or beat up a monkey, hear us out.)

Dr. Phillip Johnson says that as long as you're talking about evolution as "a gradual process by which one kind of living creature changes into something different," then evolution doesn't contradict God, your parents, or your Sunday school teacher. This is called "microevolution."

Microevolution and Natural Selection

Microevolution simply refers to minor variations that occur in populations of people or animals over time. Over the years, the human race has gotten taller, and we live a lot longer than people used to live. That's because of better nutrition and better working conditions. You could say that we humans have *evolved* into larger and longer-living people. In the same way, animals adapt to their surroundings and gradually change in the process. This is *micro-evolution*.

You will also hear a term called "natural selection". This also happens in populations of people or animals over time. Phillip Johnson writes that natural selection "has an effect in maintaining the genetic fitness of a population." Creatures with genetic defects or inferior genetic features do not survive to reproduce and therefore do not leave descendants. A good example of this would be a giraffe born with a short neck. Since giraffes eat from tall trees, giraffes with tall necks survive, while those with short necks don't. Over the years, only the long-necked giraffes survive to reproduce, leading to more giraffes with long necks, not short ones. This is *natural selection.*

On the other hand, if by evolution you mean that a fish evolves into a lizard, and a lizard evolves into a lemur, and a lemur evolves into a chimpanzee, and a chimpanzee evolves into Bill Gates, then you are way off, and so is your biology teacher. This is called *macroevolution*, which is at the heart of *Darwinist evolution*.

Macroevolution and Darwinism

Charles Darwin wasn't the first guy to come up with the idea that everything evolved from some kind of pre-biotic soup into the complex and intricately designed universe we have before us today, but he sure made that idea popular. Actually, Darwin didn't say how the soup got here in the first place (basically because he didn't know), but he did write a book called *On the Origin of Species* in which he explained how all the animals and humans got here. People usually refer to this as the theory of evolution, but we prefer *Darwinism* or *Darwinist evolution*, because it's a better description.

Because microevolution does occur, you don't want to say that you don't believe in evolution. What you want to say is that you don't believe in *Darwinist evolution*. Why? Because Darwinists claim that natural selection does much more than weed out the weak. Darwinists believe that natural selection and random mutation can explain all the diverse and complex living organisms that exist. Dr. Johnson explains that this is a "building effect so powerful that it can begin with a bacterial cell and gradually craft its descendants over billions of years to produce such wonders as trees, flowers, ants, birds, and humans."

Fish evolved into amphibians, which evolved into reptiles, which evolved into birds and mammals. Furthermore, humans and modern apes share a common ancestry (there's Uncle Curious George again). Macroevolution includes changes above the species level, especially new phyla or classes. This is what Darwinist evolution is all about.

In Chapter 5, we showed you that the animals appeared on the earth in a certain order because that's the way God created them. On the sixth day of creation, God went wild with this huge burst of animal life (remember the Cambrian Explosion?). To this day scientists scratch their heads over the Cambrian Explosion. They can't explain it. On the other hand, people who believe that God was the First Cause and Intelligent Designer of the universe and all things in it know exactly what happened.

Now, the funny thing is that Darwinist evolutionists agree on the order of the Bible record. They agree with the Bible that fish (Day 5) came before birds (Day 5), which came before mammals (Day 6), which came before humans (Day 6). What they don't agree on is how all these creatures got here. Because many Darwinist evolutionists refuse to admit that an Intelligent Designer created the universe and all living creatures in an orderly fashion, they have no choice but to say that all creatures are linked together, and everything came from an impersonal beginning. Without God in the picture, all you have going for you is the link.

The Truth about the Link

You've heard about the missing link, right? This is the magic connection Darwinist evolutionists have been looking for. You see, for nearly a century and a half scientists have been digging and scratching and searching for some kind of link between different species. Mostly they've been looking for a link between monkeys, apes, and humans. You would think that by now some-one somewhere would have found something. But guess what? They've got nothing. Zip. Zero. Nada. There is no missing link, and there never will be.

If You Can't Find It, Why Not Fake It?

Scientists have been so anxious to find the missing link that at times their science has not been very good. In fact, at times it's been downright dishonest. An English lawyer and amateur geologist by the name of Charles Dawson found some fossils in England that he thought were from the missing link, and he took them to officials at the British Museum for examination. In 1912, the scientists announced that they had found the missing link. His name was Piltdown man. For more than forty years they didn't let anyone else examine this famous fossil, so everyone pretty much accepted the "fact" that there was a link between apes and man. There was only one problem. The link was a fake, and the British scientists knew it.

John Wiester writes that "some unknown person with a good bit of scientific knowledge had taken the jaw of an ape and the skull of a man and cleverly doctored them to fit the scientific expectation of what the missing link should look like." Can you believe that? The sad part is that for more than forty years, students just like you were told that according to the "evidence," we came from monkeys. Even worse, school textbooks continued to tell the story of Piltdown man for years after the rascal was exposed.

The Truth about Monkeys

"But what about the monkey fossils that are real?" you might be asking (if you aren't asking, you should). No problem. Scientists have found fossils that were real primates, like *Ramapithecus*, an ape-like creature that lived around 12 million years ago. As much as some scientists would like to believe that this guy was our ancestor, there just isn't any proof that he was the missing link. *Ramapithecus* was just what the fossil showed—an ape-like creature.

In 1974 Donald Johanson, a world-famous paleoanthropologist (that's a guy who studies human ancestors), discovered "Lucy," also known as *Australopithecus afarensis*. A lot of people thought that Lucy was the missing link, but again, the proof was inconclusive. Johanson himself admitted that "science has not known, and does not know today, just how or when the all-important transition from ape to hominid took place."

What's a Hominid?

Anthropologists define *hominid* as a member of the family of humans. Technically, a hominid walks on two feet and is characterized by erect posture. That means an ape is not a hominid, because an ape walks mainly on its feet and hands (kind of like you did when you crawled as a baby), and it doesn't stand erect (unless it's pounding its chest like some guys do after they score a touchdown or do something they think is great). There are fossil records of hominids (Lucy was a hominid living around 3 to 4 million years ago—but even scientists who believe in macroevolution disagree as to whether these hominids were the ancestors of man or modern-day apes).

The truth is that these ancient monkeys and ape-like creatures existed because God created them, but then they became extinct. Like we said in the last chapter, on Day 6 of creation God was in a constant state of creating and re-creating. Remember, people who believe in macroevolution have no choice but to believe in Darwinist evolution (sometimes called *naturalism*), even if the evidence points the other way.

On the other hand, if you believe that the earth and biological life owe their existence to a purposeful, intelligent Creator, then you believe that God made all things—including monkeys and humans—uniquely and for a purpose. God doesn't make mistakes—all is according to His plan. If there's a close similarity between monkeys and humans, it's because we have a common Designer, not necessarily a common ancestry. The other thing you've got in your favor by believing in intelligent design is that the more science discovers, the more science points to God, and not to Darwinist evolution.

Fred Flintstone's Grand Entrance

Have we mentioned that Day 6 was the highlight of creation? God must have been having a great time making all the swimmers and fliers and crawlers and walkers. And He made something else that you're probably wondering about: the caveman.

Okay, so maybe God didn't call these Fred and Wilma Flintstone creatures "cavemen" (we really don't know what He called them), but He definitely made them. Books and movies have given us all kinds of images about these hominids, so it's pretty hard to think of cavemen as anything but hulking, hairy beasts (kind of like Mankind or Stone Cold Austin, but without the brain and well-oiled pectoral muscles). In fact, there were two distinct hominids God created on Day 6 that probably resembled us in many ways.

The Neanderthal

This interesting-looking hominid (stocky, bulky, hairy, flat forehead, receding chin) lived between 30,000 and 100,000 years ago, and the evidence shows that Neanderthals were cave dwellers (that's where the term "caveman" came from). But Neanderthals had several human characteristics: They hunted, used tools, had some kind of language (even if it was just grunting and scratching), and gathered in groups, indicating a social order. Yet the fossil and skeletal records show that they became extinct.

The Cro-Magnon

About 35,000 years ago, Cro-Magnon came on the scene. Paleoanthropologists love Cro-Magnons, because their physical appearance was very similar to modern humans. Cro-Magnons were more intelligent than Neanderthals, and the reason we know that is because Cro-Magnons used more advanced tools. Scientists don't call Cro-Magnon the missing link. In the view of the macroevolutionist, Cro-Magnon was the immediate ancestor of *Homo sapiens* (that's us). There's only one problem. Even though Cro-Magnons had many human characteristics, including intelligence, they lacked some other qualities shared by all human beings.

"Humans are more than just intelligent. Our sense of justice, our need for aesthetic pleasure, our imaginative flights, and our penetrating self-awareness, all combine to create an indefinable spirit which I believe is the 'soul.'"

—Richard Leakey, paleoanthropologist

The Caveman Comes Up Short

Cavemen may be the pride of paleoanthropologists, but they were not humans in the truest sense of the word. What sets us human beings apart from cavemen and all other animals is our spiritual nature. Dr. Hugh Ross lists these five characteristics of a "spiritual component" unique to you and to all humans who have ever lived:

1. Awareness of a moral code "written" or impressed within a conscience (that means that you know when you've done the wrong thing, even if you don't admit it).
2. Concerns about death and about life after death (even people who don't believe in heaven think about life after death).
3. Desire to communicate with and worship a higher being (even people who don't go to church think about God).
4. Consciousness of self (which is why you won't leave the house until you look really good, which for us takes quite a while).
5. Capacity to recognize truth and absolutes (you know that 2+2=4, not 5).

Made in the Image of God

Darwinist evolutionists have never been able to explain why human beings have this spiritual nature (or "soul"). We are the only creatures who have ever had these characteristics. If we evolved from lower life forms, then somewhere along the way you would think there would be a list of Monkey Commandments, or evidence of a First Orangutan Church, or some kind of Cro-Magnon Constitution that says all hominids are created equal. But there's nothing. Just like there is no fossil evidence that we descended from the apes, there's no evidence that any other creatures have ever possessed a moral code or a spiritual nature. We are unique in the world.

Darwinists can't explain how this happened, but the Bible does. Very clearly. Look what it says in Genesis (keep in mind that it's still Day 6):

> Then God said, "Let us make people in our image, to be like our-selves. They will be masters over all life—the fish in the sea, the birds in the sky, and all the livestock, wild animals, and small animals. So God created people in his own image; God patterned them after him-self; male and female he created them. (Genesis 1:26–27)

This is very, very huge! After spending five and a half days creating the heavens and the earth and all the land and water and plant life and fish and birds and animals—God did something completely different. He created people, and He created them "in his own image." This was a first for God. He didn't create anything else in His own image. Adam and Eve were the first. We are a separate, distinct, and completely unique creation. We are a first edition, not a copy.

So Do We Look Like God?

Nobody has ever seen God, so you couldn't say we look like Him. That's not what "the image of God" means. What it means is that we have God's imprint. We are His design. And because God's imprint is in every human being, every human being has no choice but to think about God. The Bible says:

> For the truth about God is known to them instinctively. God has put this knowledge in their hearts. From the time the world was created, people have seen the earth and sky and all that God made. They can clearly see his invisible qualities—his eternal power and divine nature. So they have no excuse whatsoever for not knowing God. (Romans 1:19–20)

As you're going to see in the next chapter, the implications for this image of God business are gigantic.

* No other creatures can communicate openly and intelligently with God, but we can and do, because we are made in God's image.
* No other creatures have been given the responsibility to manage the earth's resources and its animals, but we have, because we are made in God's image.
* No other creatures have the ability to obey or disobey God, but we do, because we are made in God's image.

God and Your DNA

The greatest scientific discoveries of the last few years are all about your DNA, that sequence of chromosomes that contains the "information code" that makes you who you are. Scientists are just now beginning to understand how complex and amazing the DNA code really is. The more we learn about our DNA (it's called "mapping"), the more we see that it did not come about by accident. Just as there was an intelligent design for the universe, there was an intelligent design for you, and it all starts with your DNA. As King David wrote in the Psalms, we are "fearfully and wonderfully made."

So What?

So what does all of this mean, especially when this stuff starts coming up in school?

1. Evolution isn't evil. Evolution happens, but only when you're talking about *microevolution*, which refers to minor variations that occur in populations over time.

2. On the other hand, *Darwinist evolution* (or *macroevolution*) claims that some "undirected mechanistic process" can explain all the diverse and complex living organisms that exist. There was no purposeful, personal, intelligent designer.

3. In the whole issue of humans and apes sharing a common ancestry, science cannot explain how or when or even *IF* the transition from apes to humans took place.

4. There is evidence that hominids such as Neanderthals and Cro-Magnons possessed some human characteristics, but they lacked the qualities that make us humans unique.

5. As humans, we are unique because we are created in the image of God. We literally have God's imprint in our lives.

Chapter 7

Why It All Matters

We hope you have gotten many of your questions answered about dinosaurs, cavemen, and UFO's. While those are interesting questions, now let's talk about some really important stuff. You see, this whole business about how the world (and the human race) began is more significant than just satisfying your curiosity about *Tyrannosaurus rex*, Cro-Magnons, and space aliens. The most important part about how the world began is . . . YOU!

You're Special (and we're not just saying that)

For years, your mother has been telling you that you are special. But you might not have believed it. Moms have to say things like that. It's in the *New Mother's Handbook* that the hospital gave her on the day you were born. (Speaking of that day, your mom probably also said that you were the cutest baby ever born. But can you really believe that

statement? Take a look at one of
your newborn baby pictures. All
you'll see is a bunch of pinkish
wrinkles with a crooked smile,
and that is just your bottom.)

But your mom was right, as
moms usually are (although she
was exaggerating about your baby
cuteness). You *are* special. Your DNA
proves that you are unique. There is no one else like you. God created you as one of a kind. (We know that we talked about this in
Chapter 6, but we thought we ought to say it again just in case you
were dozing off back then.)

Don't overlook the significance of this. This is huge. You aren't just
some meaningless link in the evolutionary chain. You aren't just a
freak of nature (even though your older sister may call you that). In
fact, you are way more special than you might realize.

You've Got a Lot in Common with God

Because you are a human (which we're assuming), you are special
because you have characteristics of God Himself. Let's look back to
Genesis 1:27 for a moment:

> *So God created people in his own image; God patterned them after
> himself.*

Wow! God made you like Himself. He didn't do that with the jellyfish, or the monkeys, or even the cavemen. Nope! It is humans, and
only humans, that are created in God's image. This means that:

* **You're going to live forever.** That is pretty amazing, isn't it?
  Every other thing in the universe is going to die. The sun will
  eventually burn out. The plants will wither. Fish die and

decompose on the ocean floor (unless they are goldfish, and then they get flushed down the toilet). The wild animals grow old and die (or die and get eaten; or get shot and stuffed and mounted on the wall in some rustic mountain lodge). We could go on, but you get the idea. Death is a certainty, except in the case of humans. Since we are made in the image of God, our spirits live forever. They are eternal, just like God's. Our physical body may start breaking down and falling apart (and if you need proof of this, just listen to your dad grunt when he bends down to tie his shoelaces), but our spirits live on after the funeral is over. Our spirits live forever.

* **You've Got a Soul.** You have a spiritual nature that allows you to connect with the creator of the universe. No other animals or creatures have this ability. (About the closest they get is when a dog howls at the moon.) You can know God's thoughts (through the Holy Spirit and by reading the Bible). And you can have conversations with God (through prayer). This means that your life can be a real adventure. All of the other creations in the world have a pretty boring existence (there isn't much excitement in being a snail or broccoli), but *you* get the chance to be interactive with God.

* **You Have the Potential to Have Some of God's Characteristics.** We doubt that God will give you the power to create your own universe, or to walk on water, but He wants you to have some of His personality traits.

    ✓ God is truth (Romans 3:4), and He wants you to be truthful.
    ✓ God is love (1 John 4:7–9), and He wants you to love Him and love others.
    ✓ God is forgiving (Romans 5:15), and He wants you to forgive other people who have been mean to you.

God's personality is usually just the opposite of our natural reactions. As humans, we usually are quick to lie and argue and hold a grudge. We may not want to be this way, but it is difficult to stop these natural instincts. But the people who have believed in God and put Him in charge of their lives have the Holy Spirit living within them. The Holy Spirit has the power to bring completely different qualities to your life. Here is the Bible's list of identifiable characteristics of the Holy Spirit, called "the fruit of the Spirit," as found in Galatians 5:22–23:

✓ Love   ✓ Goodness

✓ Joy   ✓ Faithfulness

✓ Peace   ✓ Gentleness

✓ Patience   ✓ Self-control

✓ Kindness

And there are more character traits of the Holy Spirit mentioned elsewhere in the Bible. Now, even though you might be a really great kid, we're sure you'll agree that it would take God's supernatural power to show these kinds of characteristics in your life all the time. But that's exactly what can happen if you let God assume control of your life—which means you'll have some of His own characteristics. (By the way, this is further proof that God created humans specially and separately from the animal kingdom. The fruits of the Spirit can only grow in people. You never hear about the kindness of a pit bull dog or the self-control of a great white shark.)

Hmmm . . . living forever, being able to talk with God, and being like Him. All of that seems to make you a pretty amazing person.

You're Going out of This World

We want to tell you something else incredible about yourself. Remember when we talked about your living forever? (You ought to remember it because it was only a few pages ago.) Well, that will really happen. Actually, it has already. It has been going on for as many years as you are old. And up to this point, you have been living all of those years here on the earth. (We're assuming you haven't been on any of those Space Shuttle trips yet.) But most of the "forever" part won't be here on Earth.

The Bible says that after you're done using your physical body, you're going to be living with God or without Him. There are two different places where this will happen:

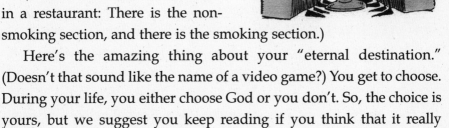

* Heaven is the place where God lives.
* Hell is the place where He doesn't.

(Think of them as two sections in a restaurant: There is the non-smoking section, and there is the smoking section.)

Here's the amazing thing about your "eternal destination." (Doesn't that sound like the name of a video game?) You get to choose. During your life, you either choose God or you don't. So, the choice is yours, but we suggest you keep reading if you think that it really doesn't matter.

You Ain't Seen Nothing Yet

Heaven and hell are real places. We aren't talking about some fairy-tale, imaginary land like Luke Skywalker's visit to Yoda in Degobah or Harry Potter's adventures at Hogwarts. These places are real, and the Bible describes them in great detail.

Here's a brief description of what heaven will be like:

* Heaven is a place so incredibly beautiful that there is nothing like it on Earth. Think of your favorite beach or ski slope. That place is a dump compared to heaven.

* Heaven won't be boring. So, don't think that you'll just sit on a cloud, flapping your wings, shining your halo, and strumming on a harp (just the old hymns; nothing contemporary). It won't be that way at all. You are going to be excited the entire time that you are there (which will be the rest of forever). There won't be any sadness in heaven, so we're pretty sure that you'll be doing exactly what you want to be doing (which probably leaves out homework and chores).

* Best of all, heaven will be the place where you will be in the presence of God. We can't describe that to you because we can't even imagine how awesome that is going to be. We get kind of excited and nervous when we meet a professional athlete or a celebrity. If you can get goose bumps at the thought of golfing a round with Tiger Woods or practicing soccer kicks with Michelle Akers, don't you think that being face to face with God will be unbelievably awesome? And you don't just get to *meet* Him; the two of you can hang out together for the rest of eternity.

Now, get ready for a major switch. Here is what hell will be like:

* Think of the worst place on earth. Hell will be worse...much worse.

* The Bible uses words like "lake of fire" and "place of torment" to describe hell. No matter how you read it, that sounds miserable.

* The Bible also talks about the inhabitants of hell being in pain and agony. It says that there will be "gnashing of teeth." We aren't sure what "gnashing" involves, but it doesn't sound good.

* Worst of all, God won't be there. When you take Him out of the picture, everything is bleak.

Here is an important thing to remember about heaven and hell:

If you are going to end up in heaven, then your time on Earth is as bad as your life will ever be. But if you are going to end up in hell, then your time on Earth is as good as your life is ever going to get.

You might wonder why we are going into such detail about heaven and hell in a book about how the world got started. Simple. What you think about how the world began influences what you think about how your life will end.

What You Think about How the World Began Is Important for Your Future

In Chapter 2, we talked about two opposing views of the world. Either God is in it, or He isn't. In the context of thinking about the beginning of the world, the two world-views are expressed this way: Either God created the world, or He didn't.

Believe it or not, what people believe about the beginning of the world will determine what they believe about heaven and hell. Let us show you how that happens. We'll start with someone who believes that everything just happened by chance (the Darwinist evolutionists).

If you think that the World Began By chance, then . . .

* It is silly to believe in God (because He doesn't exist).
* You don't have to make any decision about God during your life.
* When you die, you're just dead. Nothing else happens—except maybe your decaying body is worm food.
* There is no heaven and hell.

But if you think that God created the world, then . . .

* He exists, so you better find out about Him.
* He has a plan for the world (in general) and for you (in particular), and you better find out about it.
* You must decide whether you want to follow God's plan for your life.
* What you decide about God will determine your "eternal destination" (and that ain't no video game).

Just in case you were wondering what world-view God wants you to have, He left you a little clue in Jeremiah 29:11:

> *"For I know the plans I have for you," says the* LORD. *"They are plans for good and not for disaster, to give you a future and a hope."*

So, you see, you need to come to some conclusion about the beginning of the world so you can make your decisions about how you are going to spend your future. (And when we say "future," we aren't talking about what you want to do on next summer's vacation. We're talking your forever future.)

An End to Beginnings

When you started reading this book, we didn't know you very well. But that has certainly changed, hasn't it? We have been through quite a bit together now.

* We survived the big bang, and we stuck together for those billions of years as the galaxies spread across the skies.
* We also hung with each other during the millions of years while the atmosphere changed on planet Earth.

* We even avoided being hit by droppings from that 150-pound flying reptile.

All of that has been quite a bonding experience for us.

Now that we know you so well, we're sorry that this book has got to end. But it does. You're ready to move on to much deeper thoughts about God, and the world, and yourself.

We've tried our best to give you an overview of how the world got started. With all of the scientific evidence that we have examined:

* We sure hope you've determined that God was the One who got it all started and has been involved every step of the way.
* And we hope that you have developed a world-view with God in charge.

(Consider that as a souvenir of our travels together.)

But most of all, we hope that you are more fully convinced than ever that the Bible's report of the beginning of the world is totally believable!

So What?

Betcha thought you were done with this book. Not so fast! We've got a little more to share with you, and we think this may be the most important part of the whole book. Here's why:

You can read a book like this and learn a lot (we hope you have). The problem is that most of what you learn from books goes directly into your *head*, where it sits for a little while and then leaks out your various head holes as new stuff comes in. It's part of human nature.

The only way to avoid losing the important stuff that comes into your head—such as the information in this book—is to send it from your *head* to your *heart*. The way you do that is to believe that the information could change the way you live. Another way to look at it is this:

Knowledge Becomes valuable to you when it goes from Being information in your head to Being emotion in your heart.

At the end of several chapters, we put in a little section called "So What?" We wanted to show you how the information related to your life. Now we're going to go a little deeper and show you how this stuff can change your life.

So What Does This All Mean?

We've been dealing with some pretty amazing things—God, the big bang, dinosaurs, cavemen, life on other planets, beans in your nose—and what God has to do with all of them. We discovered together that God didn't just begin everything, but He was also involved every step of the way to give us the incredible "just right" universe we enjoy today.

This isn't just us talking. The Bible—God's totally reliable and personal message to you—lays everything out in an orderly, elegant way. The story of creation as told in the Bible is more than a story. It's the truth, and the more we learn about God's universe, the more the universe points to God.

From Your Head to Your Heart

Okay, so much for the information in your head. Now let's get to your heart. How does knowing that "in the beginning God created the heavens and the earth" make a difference in your heart? Here are a couple of verses from the Bible to help you "internalize" the information:

He is the God who made the world and everything in it. Since he is Lord of heaven and earth, he doesn't live in man-made temples, and

human hands can't serve his needs—for he has no needs. He himself gives life and breath to everything, and he satisfies every need there is. (Acts 17:24–25)

This should give you tremendous confidence in the God who loves you. He wants to meet your every need, when you need it, for your own good. Jesus said:

Your heavenly Father already knows all your needs, and he will give you all you need from day to day if you live for him and make the Kingdom of God your primary concern. (Matthew 6:32–33)

When all this information about creation and intelligent design goes from your head to your heart, you will begin to trust God for all your needs. The same God who created the world and made you in His image has promised to get you through the day, the week, the year—and your entire life. He is the 24/7 God who will never leave you.

What We Learned from Some Very Smart People

Just as we were finishing this book, we contacted two very prominent scientists to get their opinions about the universe and how it got here. These guys are very smart. In fact, one of them was a physicist who worked on a project that measured the beginning of the universe. The other guy was an astronomer who received this little award called the Nobel prize (maybe you've heard of it).

We were thinking of you when we talked to them. We asked each of them if it was possible to combine belief in God with the evidence of science. (Keep in mind that neither one claimed to believe in God.)

The physicist who has measured the beginning of the universe said that it's going to take "twenty or thirty years" for this information to really sink in. Whenever great scientific discoveries are made, he explained, it always takes a while for the truth of those discoveries to impact the culture (which includes your school).

Think about that for a minute. Science has just in the last few years confirmed that the universe had a beginning. Don't get discouraged that you're still being taught something different. It's going to take some time. But when the implications of the evidence begin to sink in (think of it going from the head to the heart), then we could very well be looking at a dramatic change in the way this stuff is taught in school.

The Nobel prize guy explained that the job of science is to explain what the universe is like and how it works. On the other hand, the job of religion is to understand the meaning and purpose of the universe. With all that is happening in science lately, his view was that the two— science and religion—will eventually come together, as long as we understand them both well enough.

What You Can Do with What You Know

We've got to tell you that our hearts were stirred as we listened to these scientists. Now we want to stir your heart with a challenge. If you have any interest in science, whether it's physics, biology, astronomy, or any of the sciences—we encourage you to study and learn and do all you can to become the best science student you can.

Who knows? Maybe God is calling you to become a scientist so you can have an impact on the world in the years ahead. Don't shy away from science. Let God use you to tell His story in your school, in your college, and in your profession. Don't just rely on what others have told you. Learn for yourself. Ask God to open your head and your heart to His truth.

Don't think for a minute that we have learned all we can about the universe and how it works. The discoveries that will be made in the next years will continue to "tell of the glory of God" (Psalm 19:1). Wouldn't it be exciting to be a part of that?

If science isn't exactly your strong point, don't worry. Neither of us was trained in science, but we learned on our own. And here's what our knowledge did for us. It gave us a much greater appreciation of God the Creator. Our love for Him has deepened (it's gone to our hearts) because we better understand how much He cares for us.

We hope you experience that for yourself, and we hope you tell some other people along the way.

Books We Had to Read before We Wrote Ours

Someone once said that an expert isn't someone who knows everything (that's called a "know-it-all"). An expert is someone who knows who to ask. If that's true, then we almost qualify as experts, because we did a lot of asking, mainly through the following books and Web sites. These authors are very smart, especially the One who wrote the Bible.

BOOKS

American Scientific Affiliation. *Teaching Science in a Climate of Controversy.* Ipswich, Massachusetts: American Scientific Affiliation, 1986.

Ankerberg, John, and Weldon, John. *Darwin's Leap of Faith.* Eugene, Oregon: Harvest House Publishers, 1998.

Behe, Michael J. *Darwin's Black Box: The Biochemical Challenge to Evolution.* New York, New York: Simon & Schuster Inc., 1998.

Crawford, Jean Burke, ed. *Planet Earth.* Alexandria, Virginia: Time-Life Books, 1997.

Davis, Percival, and Kenyon, Dean H. *Of Pandas and People.* Dallas, Texas: Haughton Publishing Company, 1999.

Dembski, William A., ed. *Intelligent Design.* Downers Grove, Illinois: InterVarsity Press, 1999.

Dembski, William A., ed. *Mere Creation: Science, Faith & Intelligent Design.* Downers Grove, Illinois: InterVarsity Press, 1998.

Denton, Michael. *Evolution: A Theory in Crisis.* Chevy Chase, Maryland: Adler & Adler Publishers, Inc., 1986.

Eichenberger, Jim. *No Accident, No Apologies: Helping Teens Understand the Creation/Evolution Debate.* Cincinnati, Ohio: Standard Publishing, 1998.

Fischer, Robert B. *God Did It, But How?* Ipswich, Massachusetts: ASA Press, 1997.

Furniss, Tim. *Fantastic Facts about Stars & Planets.* Bath, England: Dempsey Parr, 2000.

Futato, Mark D. *Creation: A Witness to the Wonder of God.* Phillipsburg, New Jersey: P&R Publishing, 2000.

God. *The Holy Bible,* New Living Translation. Wheaton, Illinois: Tyndale Publishing House, 1996.

Hannegraaff, Hank. *The Face that Demonstrates the Farce of Evolution.* Nashville, Tennessee: Word Publishing, 1998.

Hayward, Alan. *Creation and Evolution.* Minneapolis, Minnesota: Bethany House Publishers, 1995.

Heeren, Fred. *Show Me God.* Wheeling, Illinois: Day Star Publications, 2000.

Jeeves, Malcolm A. and Berry, R.J. *Science, Life and Christian Belief.* Grand Rapids, Michigan: Baker Books, 1998.

Johnson, Phillip E. *Darwin on Trial.* Downers Grove, Illinois: InterVarsity Press, 1993.

Johnson, Phillip E. *Defeating Darwinism by Opening Minds.* Downers Grove, Illinois: InterVarsity Press, 1997.

Johnson, Phillip E. *Objections Sustained: Subversive Essays on Evolution, Law and Culture.* Downers Grove, Illinois: InterVarsity Press, 1998.

Johnson, Phillip E. *Reason in the Balance: The Case against Naturalism in Science, Law and Education.* Downers Grove, Illinois: InterVarsity Press, 1995.

Moreland, J.P. *The Creation Hypothesis: Scientific Evidence for an Intelligent Designer.* Downers Grove, Illinois: InterVarsity Press, 1994.

Moreland, J.P., and Reynolds, John Mark. *Three Views on Creation and Evolution.* Grand Rapids, Michigan: Zondervan Publishing House, 1999.

Muncaster, Ralph O. *Science: Was the Bible ahead of Its Time?* Eugene, Oregon: Harvest House Publishers, 2000.

Richards, Larry. *It Couldn't Just Happen.* Dallas, Texas: Word Publishing, 1989.

Ross, Hugh. *Beyond the Cosmos: The Extra-Dimensionality of God.* Colorado Springs, Colorado: NavPress Publishing Group, 1996.

Ross, Hugh. *Creation and Time.* Colorado Springs, Colorado: NavPress Publishing Group, 1994.

Ross, Hugh. *The Creator and the Cosmos: How the Greatest Scientific Discoveries of the Century Reveal God.* Colorado Springs, Colorado: NavPress Publishing Group, 1993.

Ross, Hugh. *The Fingerprint of God.* New Kensington, Pennsylvania: Whitaker House, 1989.

Ross, Hugh. *The Genesis Question.* Colorado Springs, Colorado: NavPress Publishing Group, 1998.

Sailhamer, John. *Genesis Unbound.* Sisters, Oregon: Multnomah Books, 1996.

Schroeder, Gerald L. *Genesis and the Big Bang.* New York, New York: Bantam Books, 1992.

Schroeder, Gerald L. *The Science of God.* New York, New York: Broadway Books, 1997.

Sproul, R.C. *Not a Chance.* Grand Rapids, Michigan: Baker Books, 1994.

Wiester, John. *The Genesis Connection.* Nashville, Tennessee: Thomas Nelson Publishers, 1983.

Wiester, John. *What's Darwin Got to Do with It?* Downers Grove, Illinois: InterVarsity Press, 2000.

Zeman, Anne, and Kelly, Kate. *Everything You Need to Know about Science Homework.* New York, New York: Scholastic Inc., 1997.

Comic Books

Ross, Hugh, and Bundschuh, Rick. *Destination: Creation.* Pasadena, California: Reasons to Believe, 1997.

Web Sites

www.britannica.com
www.daystarcom.org
www.discovery.com
www.reasons.org